In Thy Light
We See Light

lucem

The Valparaiso University Prayer Book

The 150th Anniversary
Celebration Edition

William O. Karpenko II, Editor

June 2008

*This Prayer Book
is dedicated to
the Valparaiso University Guild
and the thousands of women
whose enthusiastic and selfless actions
over the years have done much
to enhance student life on campus*

On the cover: Western view of the east side of the nave of Valparaiso University's Chapel of the Resurrection at dusk. Photo used with permission of Robert Wehmeier ('88)

All photos were taken on the Valparaiso University Campus and adjacent surroundings.

ISBN 0-9712294-2-2
ISBN 13 978-0-9712294-2-6

First printing June 2008
10,000 copies in print

Published by Valparaiso University

In Thy Light we celebrate 150 years

Eternal, ever-present God...

Whether a day, a year, 150 years or eternity, you are the Alpha and the Omega; the one who created all in the beginning; the one who sustains all today; and the one who waits to welcome all.

Your spirit was present in those men and women who sought to honor and learn of you in 1859. Your spirit hovered over the glories and struggles of those leaders keen to make inspired contributions. Their cherished names now live in Valparaiso University history books.

Your spirit was present in those Lutheran laity and clergy who in 1925 dreamed of a place to equip their sons and daughters for lofty endeavors in church and society. Your spirit steadied in times of depression, worldwide war, civil rights movements, denominational strife, burgeoning technology, ever-increasing change, and leadership transition.

It is in Thy Light that we now celebrate 150 years, a Light that engages the mind, that moves the heart, that lifts the spirit, and brings all together in common endeavor and service.

It is in Thy Light that we now look to a future full of learning that edifies, writing that enlightens, and teaching that inspires. Kindle in us trust in Jesus Christ, who was with you in the beginning and whose life, death, and resurrection light our way today and until you welcome us home. Amen.

William O. Karpenko II

3

Table of Contents

Praying in the Light

This is the message we have heard from him and proclaim to you, that God is light and in him there is no darkness at all. If we say that we have fellowship with him while we are walking in darkness, we lie and do not do what is true; but if we walk in the light as he himself is in the light, we have fellowship with one another, and the blood of Jesus his Son cleanses us from all sin. 1 John 1:5-7 NRSV[1]

These words capture the title of this prayer book. As we walk with Jesus, God's light, we are linked to one another in that glorious fellowship we call the Church. Cleansed from our sin, we take on a new identity:

But you are a chosen race, a royal priesthood, a holy nation, God's own people, in order that you may proclaim the mighty acts of him who called you out of darkness into his marvelous light.

1 Peter 2:9-10

As one of God's own people, each of us is called to convey to others, in word and deed, what God has done in our lives.

Sounds simple, right? Not really, when darkness relentlessly invades, captivates, and enslaves. Even when we know how God wishes us to live, we slip back into dismal, dire, and defeating ways of living.

Still, God's light beckons. Jesus welcomes. Life in him enlightens, enlivens, and engages us in serving our neighbor.

The way ahead is bright. Even when twists in the road distress, you have the prayers of God's people in these pages. In Christ's light, you will see all the light you need to do God's bidding today and throughout your years.

[1]Unless noted, all Scripture quotations in this prayer book are from the New Revised Standard Version Bible, copyright 1989, Division of Christian Education of the National Council of Churches of Christ in the United States of America. Used by permission. All rights reserved.

Praying with the Light

Think of this prayer book as a trusted
conversation partner: a partner that is familiar
yet capable of surprising, calming yet stimulating,
comfortable yet capable of challenging; a companion you want
to be with in the grandest of times and in the depths of despair.

As a trusted partner, this prayer book can speak to various needs
you or your friends may have. For example, if you:

- Wish a morning and evening prayer pattern, explore the
  themes for each day of the week on pages 12-25.
- Are confronting a chronic concern or issue, seek out the
  devotional pattern on pages 124-141.
- Desire to bask in the poignant and timeless wisdom of much-
  loved prayers, turn to pages 172-197.
- Want a virtual tour of Christian imagery located throughout
  campus, and adjacent surroundings, check out the photos
  on the top right-hand page corners.
- Love the rhythm of the church year, ponder the seasonal
  meditations on pages 144-169.
- Seek to be edified by original prayers of VU students, alumni,
  staff, and faculty, find their words on pages 32-103 and
  111-120.
- Want to explore varied ways to pray, practice the different
  approaches located before each of the six book chapters,
  pages 11, 27, 123, 143, 171, and 199.
- Welcome the earnest prayers of Christians from other
  universities, turn to pages 200-207; or
- List those campus happenings and individuals you would like
  to pray for on a regular basis on pages 121 and 214-215.

Beyond these opportunities for trusted conversation, may this
book spark you to respond to the Light – Jesus Christ – who can
illumine your way today, tomorrow, and throughout your life.

SEEKING THE LIGHT IN PRAYER
Readying ourselves

Just as people vary in their approaches to communication, so it is with how people pray. Some prefer to pray in silence, others pray out loud. Some pray the words of Scripture, while others verbalize what's on their minds.

St. Paul encourages those who follow Jesus to "pray without ceasing" (I Thessalonians 5:17), and so it happens as we continually turn to God in word and thought with praising, leading, wondering, thanking, and remembering.

Still, one of the hardest things about praying is taking the first step. Even though the present never seems quite right, and there may never be a perfect time to pray, keep these ideas in mind:

1. God is ever-near, desiring as your dear Father to hear and respond to your heartfelt thoughts and feelings. (Matthew 6)

2. God knows you as no one else and understands even your unspoken groaning, longings, and pleading. (Romans 8)

3. While you are encouraged to "ask, search, knock" (Matthew 7), one does so, trusting that God's will, not yours, be done.

4. You have a profound prayer ally in the Holy Spirit, who will help you offer the words and surrender yourself to God. (John 16)

5. Remember that the blessings that come from prayer are not earned but, rather, are gifts from God.

6. If it helps you pray, set aside a special place and a special time; if you tend to pray on the run, or as the Spirit incites, let that approach uplift you.

7. If you are seeking some variety in your prayer life, a different approach to prayer can be found at the beginning of each of the six chapters of this book. The first, the ancient practice of *Examen*, is on the next page.

God waits. God listens. God speaks. Relax and enter God's presence.

Promise

*I will lead the blind by a road they
do not know, by paths they have not
known I will guide them. I will turn
the darkness before them into light,
the rough places into level ground.*

ISAIAH 42:16

Purpose – *Examen* is the deliberate examination of God's presence or absence in one's life.

Practice – This practice has a long history in the Christian church. The praying of the *Examen* is meant to explore patterns of thought and behavior that lead us to or away from God. This practice is most helpful at the end of the day as one gets ready for restful sleep or as one arises and prepares for the day ahead.

Process

1. Quietly pray that the Holy Spirit help you be aware of when and where you were blessed with an awareness of Christ's presence today.

2. Ask yourself how you failed to notice Christ today and were not mindful of his presence.

3. Make a prayer of confession, if appropriate, and pray for increased awareness of Christ's presence.

4. Give thanks for the presence of God in your life and sleep peacefully or go forth into the day with the same presence.

Prayer – Ask God to make you aware of the thoughts and behaviors that lead you to God, pray for strength to shun that which leads to an absence of God. Let God, the source of life, embrace you.

Charity

Invocation

We begin a new day and week, born once again through the waters of baptism, in the name of the Father, Son, and Holy Spirit. Amen.

Scripture reading

Put on therefore, as the elect of God, holy and beloved, bowels of mercies, kindness, humbleness of mind, meekness, long-suffering; forbearing one another, and forgiving one another. . . . And above all these things put on charity, which is the bond of perfectness. And let the peace of God rule in your hearts, to the which also ye are called in one body; and be ye thankful. (Colossians 3:12-15 KJV)

A thought to ponder

Charity. To love human beings insofar as they are nothing. That is to love them as God does.

Simone Weil (1909-1943)

Prayer

By your spirit, you have called us from sleep to wakefulness and marked us with the sign of Christ's sacrifice. May his love form us throughout this new day and reveal itself in charity, as we serve you and others with thanksgiving and in so doing receive the gift of your own joy. We ask in Jesus' name. Amen.

Blessing

Enter this day in peace, trusting that your Light has come. Amen.

Charity

Invocation

We close this day in the same embrace we knew at its opening, the trustworthy hands of the One who creates, redeems, and endlessly calls us. Amen.

Scripture reading

Though I speak with the tongues of men and of angels, and have not charity, I am become as sounding brass, or a tinkling cymbal. And though I have the gift of prophecy, and understand all mysteries, and all knowledge; and though I have all faith, so that I could remove mountains, and have not charity, I am nothing.

(1 Corinthians 13:1-2 KJV)

A thought to ponder

Where there is charity and wisdom, there is neither fear nor ignorance. St. Francis of Assisi (1181-1226)

Prayer

Accept our thanks this night, O Lord, for the bounty we have received from your hand today, for the ills and evils you prevented, and for all that you have forgiven us. Watch over us this night, and tend with abundant mercy all who had no rest from their labors this day. We ask in Jesus' name. Amen.

Blessing

Restored through the gift of a Sabbath, rest this night as one buried with Christ, ready to rise with him in the glorious light of a new day. Amen.

Prudence

Prayer

Gracious God, grant us a measure of your own wisdom as we begin our week's work. Enlighten and lead us as we respond to your call, that we see to the mending of your world through taking up the cross of your Son. Strengthen us in our weakness, dispel our fears, and guide us on paths you would have us follow. We ask in Jesus' name. Amen.

Scripture reading

The LORD by wisdom founded the earth; by understanding he established the heavens; by his knowledge the deeps broke open, and the clouds drop down the dew. My child, do not let these escape from your sight: keep sound wisdom and prudence, and they will be life for your soul and adornment for your neck. Then you will walk on your way securely and your foot will not stumble.

(Proverbs 3:19-23)

A thought to ponder

Love all, trust a few,
Do wrong to none: be able for thine enemy
Rather in power than use, and keep thy friend
Under thy own life's key: be check'd for silence,
But never tax'd for speech.

William Shakespeare (1564-1616)

Blessing

Lord, bless our going out and coming in, from this time forth, forevermore. Amen.

Prudence

Scripture reading

*The wage of the righteous leads to life, the gain of the wicked to sin.
When words are many, transgression is not lacking, but the prudent
are restrained in speech. Whoever heeds instruction is on the path
to life, but one who rejects a rebuke goes astray. Lying lips conceal
hatred, and whoever utters slander is a fool. The tongue of the
righteous is choice silver; the mind of the wicked is of little worth.
The lips of the righteous feed many, but fools die for lack of sense.
The blessing of the LORD makes rich, and he adds no sorrow with it.*
(Proverbs 10:16-22)

Prayer of confession

God of all mercy, we thank you for all the gifts by which you
have sustained and protected us throughout this day, and we ask
your forgiveness on all the ways we have sinned and failed you,
despite our faithful effort and best intentions. Bring healing to
those we have harmed, let us sleep in the peace of the redeemed,
and waken us tomorrow for another day of service. In Jesus'
name we pray. Amen.

A word of comfort and absolution

*In Christ we have redemption through his blood, the forgiveness
of our trespasses, according to the riches of his grace that he lavished
on us. With all wisdom and insight he has made known to us the
mystery of his will, according to his good pleasure that he set forth
in Christ, as a plan for the fullness of time, to gather up all things
in him, things in heaven and things on earth.*   (Ephesians 1:7-10)

Justice

Scripture reading

*Even though you offer me your burnt offerings and grain offerings,
I will not accept them; and the offerings of well-being of your fatted
animals I will not look upon. Take away from me the noise of your
songs; I will not listen to the melody of your harps. But let justice
roll down like waters, and righteousness like an ever-flowing stream.*
(Amos 5:22-24)

Thoughts to ponder

Injustice anywhere is a threat to justice everywhere.
Martin Luther King, Jr. (1929-1968)

Peace is not an absence of war, it is a virtue, a state of mind,
a disposition for benevolence, confidence, justice.
Baruch Spinoza (1632-1677)

Prayer

Lord of all, by your own breath you have quickened in us the
capacities for justice and mercy. May our hearts be tuned to
each as truly as your own, and may our service to you produce
justice and kindness conformed to the pattern of your Son's,
in whose name we pray. Amen.

Blessing

Go in peace. Serve the Lord with thanksgiving!

Justice

Invocation

Wrapped in baptismal garments and clinging to the promises
made to us in the name of the Father, Son, and Holy Spirit,
we come again into God's presence at the end of a day. Be with
us, Lord, even as you have promised. Make this place and this
moment a glimpse of your gracious reign.

Scripture reading

*He has told you, O mortal, what is good; and what does the LORD
require of you but to do justice, and to love kindness, and to walk
humbly with your God?* (Micah 6:8)

A thought to ponder

I have always found that mercy bears richer fruits than strict
justice. Abraham Lincoln (1809-1865)

Prayer

Whatever seeds of justice or mercy we have sowed today,
Lord, water them, make them grow, and may the harvest bring
glory only to you. Where we have failed, and for all the ways
we have bludgeoned mercy and compounded injustice, grant
us repentant hearts. Forgive us, renew us, and send us out once
again in the days to come, ready to find our lives through losing
them in the bearing of your Son's cross. Tonight, give us restful
sleep. Tomorrow, quicken in us the restless heart of Christ
himself. In his name we pray. Amen.

Fortitude

Invocation

We awaken to a new day in your presence, O God – Father, Son, and Spirit – our fortress, our stronghold, our ever-present help. Amen.

Scripture reading

For though I am absent in body, yet I am with you in spirit, and I rejoice to see your morale and the firmness of your faith in Christ. As you therefore have received Christ Jesus the Lord, continue to live your lives in him, rooted and built up in him and established in the faith, just as you were taught, abounding in thanksgiving.

(Colossians 2:5-7)

A thought to ponder

God give me strength to face a fact though it slay me.

Thomas H. Huxley (1825-1895)

Prayer

Almighty and merciful God, we have no fortitude of body, mind, or will except these come from you. Make all we do today become a sign of your untiring love. Sustain us on the way of daily crossbearing, as we follow the calling of your justice and your mercy, through our Lord, Jesus Christ. Amen.

Blessing

"Have no fear! I am with you," says the Lord, your God. And let all the people say, "Amen!"

Fortitude

Scripture reading

*God is our refuge and strength, a very present help in trouble.
Therefore we will not fear, though the earth should change, though
the mountains shake in the heart of the sea; though its waters roar
and foam, though the mountains tremble with its tumult.*

*There is a river whose streams make glad the city of God, the holy
habitation of the Most High. God is in the midst of the city; it shall
not be moved; God will help it when the morning dawns.*

(Psalm 46:1-5)

A thought to ponder

*"My grace is sufficient for you, for my strength is made perfect
in weakness."*   God, to Paul the Apostle (2 Corinthians 12:9)

Prayer

O God, who sees all our weaknesses and knows our every fear,
forgive, we pray, the many stumblings and failings of this day.
Let us rest now in the peace of your boundless mercy. By your
Holy Spirit, renew our faith, courage, and devotion, that
tomorrow we may join once more the struggle against those
things within us, and all around us, that diminish life and
destroy your creation. In Jesus' name we pray. Amen.

Blessing

"Blessed are the meek, for they will inherit the earth."

(Matthew 5:5)

Temperance

Invocation

Through the abundance of your steadfast love, Lord, we enter your house. All the world is your holy temple. We bow before you.

Scripture reading

Now the works of the flesh are obvious: fornication, impurity, licentiousness, idolatry, sorcery, enmities, strife, jealousy, anger, quarrels, dissensions, factions, envy, drunkenness, carousing, and things like these. . . . By contrast, the fruit of the Spirit is love, joy, peace, patience, kindness, generosity, faithfulness, gentleness, and self-control. There is no law against such things. And those who belong to Christ Jesus have crucified the flesh with its passions and desires. If we live by the Spirit, let us also be guided by the Spirit.

(Galatians 5:19-25)

Prayer

God of wisdom, keep us today from all extremes. Guard our tongues, that our words might carry kindness. Curb the appetites of our eyes, ears, or bellies that might harm ourselves or others. May we receive your gifts with grateful hearts, and share them with the same spirit of generosity we have seen in your son Jesus Christ. Amen.

Blessing

Enter this day nourished by God's wisdom, sustained by God's mercy, warmed by God's love.

Temperance

Scripture reading

Be careful then how you live, not as unwise people but as wise, making the most of the time, because the days are evil. So do not be foolish, but understand what the will of the Lord is. Do not get drunk with wine, for that is debauchery; but be filled with the Spirit, as you sing psalms and hymns and spiritual songs among yourselves, singing and making melody to the Lord in your hearts, giving thanks to God the Father at all times and for everything in the name of our Lord Jesus Christ. (Ephesians 5:15-20)

A thought to ponder

Better is a dinner of herbs where love is than a fatted ox and hatred with it. (Proverbs 15:17)

Prayer

Cleanse and renew us, gracious God, for we have filled ourselves with more than we can hold. Stay our angers, calm our fears, and prick our vanity. Forgive us for all the ways we have consumed one another, and your whole creation, as though they belonged only to us. Fill us now with your peace, and let the manna of your mercy satisfy us day after day. We pray in Jesus' name. Amen.

Blessing

Surely goodness and mercy shall follow you all the days of your life. You dwell even now in the Lord's house.

Faith

Invocation

Satisfy us in the morning with your steadfast love, O Lord, that we may rejoice and be glad all our days.

Scripture reading

Now faith is the assurance of things hoped for, the conviction of things not seen. (Hebrews 11:1)

Thoughts to ponder

The great act of faith is when a man decides he is not God.
Oliver Wendell Holmes Jr. (1841 - 1935)

Jesus said to them, *". . . truly I tell you, if you have faith the size of a mustard seed, you will say to this mountain, 'Move from here to there,' and it will move; and nothing will be impossible for you."*
(Matthew 17:20)

Prayer

All through this day, O Lord, give us faith to follow in the way of your Son, Jesus Christ, bearing his cross, forgiving as he forgave, and devoting ourselves tirelessly to his work of reconciliation in the world. In his name we pray. Amen.

Blessing

May the almighty and merciful God, Father, Son, and Holy Spirit, bless and keep us this day and always. Amen.

Faith

Invocation

Come, stay with us, Lord, for it is toward evening, and the day is almost over.

Scripture reading

So we are always confident; even though we know that while we are at home in the body we are away from the Lord – for we walk by faith, not by sight. (2 Corinthians 5:6-7)

A thought to ponder

I believe that I cannot by my own reason or strength believe in Jesus Christ, my Lord, or come to Him; but the Holy Ghost has called me by the Gospel, enlightened me with His gifts, sanctified and kept me in the true faith; even as He calls, gathers, enlightens, and sanctifies the whole Christian Church on earth, and keeps it with Jesus Christ in the one true faith; in which Christian Church He forgives daily and richly all sins to me and all believers, and at the last day will raise up me and all the dead, and will give to me and to all believers in Christ everlasting life. This is most certainly true.

> Martin Luther's explanation of the third article
> of the Apostles' Creed

Prayer

Lord, we believe. Help us this night in our unbelief. Cling to us, most especially when we cannot cling to you. In the name of Jesus. Amen.

Blessing

Into your hands we commend our spirits, for you have redeemed us, O God, our faithful God.

Hope

Invocation

Morning by morning, O God, our hope is in you.

Scripture reading

Truly the eye of the LORD is on those who fear him, on those who hope in his steadfast love, to deliver their soul from death, and to keep them alive in famine. Our soul waits for the LORD; he is our help and shield. Our heart is glad in him, because we trust in his holy name. Let your steadfast love, O LORD, be upon us, even as we hope in you. (Psalm 33:18-22)

A thought to ponder

If you lose hope, somehow you lose the vitality that keeps life moving, you lose that courage to be, that quality that helps you go on in spite of it all. And so today I still have a dream.
Martin Luther King, Jr. (1929-1968)

Prayer

Fill us with hope, O God, that in all we do this day we may act in the humble confidence that you shall attend to the ultimate end and success of all our endeavors, for we can do nothing without you. In Jesus' name. Amen.

Blessing

May the God of hope fill you with all joy and peace in believing, so that you may abound in hope by the power of the Holy Spirit.

Hope

Invocation

Let our prayers rise before you as incense, O Lord, and the
lifting up of our hands as the evening sacrifice.

Scripture reading

*For in hope we were saved. Now hope that is seen is not hope.
For who hopes for what is seen? But if we hope for what we do not
see, we wait for it with patience. Likewise the Spirit helps us in our
weakness; for we do not know how to pray as we ought, but that
very Spirit intercedes with sighs too deep for words.*

(Romans 8:24-26)

A thought to ponder

Nothing worth doing is completed in our lifetime; therefore,
we are saved by hope.   Reinhold Niebuhr (1892-1971)

Prayer

We have no hope, O God, except in you. By your mercy, forgive
us this day's sins and all our lapses in faith, hope, and love.
Heal those we have harmed, encourage those we have left
fearful, and watch faithfully over those we have forgotten.
Cleanse us in your redeeming flood, and prepare us to worship,
love, and serve you tomorrow. We ask in Jesus' name. Amen.

Blessing

Grant us, almighty and merciful God, a restful night and a
blessed end. Amen.

promise

Your word is a lamp to my feet and a light to my path.

PSALM 119:105

Purpose – Praying the Scriptures allow for devotional interaction with the Word of God.

Practice – Augustine, Luther, and others discovered the joy of simply praying the Scriptures rather than only studying them. This practice allows the Holy Spirit to "speak" and teach as one prays.

Process

1. Identify a section of the Bible to pray, such as the Psalms. You may also use a recording and listen to the text rather than reading it.

2. Find a quiet place away from distractions and quietly read or listen to the selected text.

3. Pause now and then to reflect on the text and write observations, thoughts and prayers in this prayer book or some other devotional resource.

4. Conclude by giving thanks to God for the gift of God's Word and the inspiration offered through its sacred pages.

Prayer – Pray that the Holy Spirit open your heart that it may "burn" with fervor and understanding as God's Word is revealed to you.

A president's prayer for Valparaiso University as he departs

Gracious God, your boundless grace is evident as I reflect upon all that Valparaiso University has and will become. I thank you for the wise guidance and loving support I have experienced during my tenure as president. I am also particularly grateful of all who have included me and the university in their prayers these past 20 years.

Your goodness is evident in the members of the Board of Directors. I thank you for instilling in them a willingness to give of their time, expertise, and material blessings to further the mission of this university. Their individual and collective aspirations for VU will enable it to become even more of a beacon of sound learning and profound faith.

Your goodness is also evident in my administrative colleagues, the faculty, and members of the staff who tend to the myriad of duties and responsibilities inherent in the ongoing activities of this place. I am grateful for their diligence and expertise.

I thank you for the alumni of Valparaiso University who daily give positive witness to the nature of Valparaiso University as they engage in the vocations to which they have been called. Continue to bless them as they fulfill their responsibilities as doctors, lawyers, nurses, professors, teachers, engineers, business men and women, directors of not-for-profit agencies, leaders of Christian congregations, and members of boards of various community groups.

Over the years you have blessed this university with so many marvelous students. Thank you for all who have chosen to study here. May their investment in one another, their studies, and the life of this place bring out the best in us all.

Finally, continue to gather at this place those who are responsive to your will and committed to maintain the important role the university plays in church and society. I offer these words of prayer in the name of Christ our Lord. Amen.

Alan F. Harre
(1988-2008)

A president-elect's prayer
for Valparaiso University as he arrives

Praise and thanksgiving be yours, O creator, for the women and men who are called to this place to do your work in the world. We thank you, Lord, for the Board members and presidents, students and alumni, faculty and staff, pastors and Guild members, who have built Valparaiso University, established its traditions, grown its quality and reputation, and lived out its mission in the world. We pray that you will keep us ever mindful of their contributions, sacrifices, hopes, and dreams as we consider our university's future together.

It is you, Lord, who brought us here to study, to teach, to discover, and to contribute. We are the students, faculty, and staff who labor here. We are the alumni, Board members, and friends who support the work of Valparaiso University through our time, talent, and treasure. It is you, Lord, who gathers us, equips us for vocations, and inspires us to serve.

Gather us in, Lord. Gather us in!

We pray, O Lord, for guidance as we do your work in an increasingly uncertain society. Ours is a world evermore splintered, violent, and unjust. Our voices seem weak amidst the clamor of opinion-leaders, idols, and false prophets. We seek to discern your plans for Valparaiso University and the work that you would have us do in the world. We pray for wisdom and strength, Lord. We pray for voices that can rise above the din of this weary world. We ask you to continue to light the way as you take us from the comfort of our campus and send us into the world as workers in the city of God.

Send us out, Lord. Send us out!

We pray this in the name of our lord and savior, Jesus Christ, who brings us good news, who gathers us in and sends us out, and who lives and reigns with you and the Holy Spirit, one God, now and forever. Amen.

Mark A. Heckler
(2008-   )

SHARING THE LIGHT WITHIN THE VU COMMUNITY
Light for campus life
Faith and learning

Faith and Learning

Almighty, merciful, and all-knowing God,

You have made us in your image, capable of trusting faith and eager learning. We give you thanks for hearts and minds capable of knowledge, reason, and intellect, gifts by which you invite us into your own work of creating, mending, and finding meaning in this vast universe. Help us to understand our limits as fully as our powers, and when we stray, teach us repentance and bring us close again through the calling of your Spirit and the mercy of your Son, in whose name we pray. Amen.

A prayer for insight

Ineffable Creator...

You are proclaimed
the true font of light and wisdom,
and the primal origin
raised high beyond all things.

Pour forth a ray of your brightness
into the darkened places of my mind;
disperse from my soul the twofold darkness
into which I was born:
sin and ignorance.

Grant to me keenness of mind,
capacity to remember,
skill in learning,
subtlety to interpret,
and eloquence in speech.

May you guide the beginning of my work,
direct its progress,
and bring it to completion.

SHARING THE LIGHT WITHIN THE VU COMMUNITY
  Light for campus life
  Faith and learning

You who are true God and true Man,
Who lives and reigns,
world without end. Amen.

The start of the semester

Gracious Lord,

We offer heartfelt thanks for opportunities of mental and spiritual
growth that come with beginning a new semester. Help us to
be truly grateful for the challenges of fulfilling our intellectual
potential and, at the same time, for the broader discoveries of
community and service. Give us faith and courage to stretch
and grow, and make our way in your kingdom. We ask this
in the name of Christ, our Savior.
Amen.

As I teach

Oh Lord,

Grant understanding hearts and faithful minds to those of us
who teach. Give us the wisdom to know when to speak and when
to listen, when to lead and when to follow, when to believe in
order to find understanding, when to seek understanding in order
to believe. Keep us and our students ever mindful of the fact that
our love of learning is both a sign and a symptom of our desire
for you. Amen.

Integrating what I am learning with my faith

God of all truth,

Sometimes I wonder if it is possible to hold together what I learn
in my classes and what I call my faith. All the differing ideas,
theories, questions, and schools of thought overwhelm my mind.

33

SHARING THE LIGHT WITHIN THE VU COMMUNITY
Light for campus life
Faith and learning

Every class introduces me to some new, unique, conceptual world, and each has its own language, terms, and models.

I know that part of my calling as a university student is to re-think things, or, as I've learned to call such work, to "de-construct" my ideas and beliefs. That's all fine and sometimes it leads to valuable insights. Still, I often feel like a boat being steered by someone else, first in one direction, then quickly in another.

I need an anchor, gracious God. I need you.

I hunger for clarity, for coherence in how my faith fits with what I'm learning. Please send your Spirit to guide and, where necessary, guard me.

In Jesus' name. Amen.

Professors who profess the faith

All-knowing, ever-wise God,

I am so grateful for your ongoing presence and work in the lives of my teachers.

They are so gifted. So insightful. So able to weld together matters of faith with what we are studying.

I am grateful that you have led them to do the complex, demanding work of integrating their field of study and their intellectual passions with their own faith convictions. Help me to emulate their commitment to rigorous thinking and obedient faith.

May you lead them to know how significant an instrument of faith formation their intellectual excellence and personal witness is in my life as a student. In them, I see the Light that is Jesus Christ. In his name. Amen.

SHARING THE LIGHT WITHIN THE VU COMMUNITY
  Light for campus life
  Faith and learning

Before studying

Dear God,

I thank you for giving me the opportunity to be a student. You have allowed me to nurture my gifts so that when I graduate they can be used for your good. Still, in the busyness of campus life, I often find it difficult to concentrate on the tasks you have set before me. May I never view my studies as work, but as opportunities that you have provided for me to better myself and foster my gifts. Keep my eyes on ways that I might use what I study to serve others throughout your world. Again, thank you, God. Amen.

Facing challenging assignments

Lord,

I have received an assignment, one that challenges who I am but in the end may transform me. When Solomon became king over Israel, he prayed for wisdom. Grant me this wisdom to know your guiding hand. When you told Peter to fish again in the lake that refused to yield its produce, he did so faithfully. Enlighten my heart to see hope beyond the trial. When Gideon faced insurmountable foes with his insufficient strength, he prayed for your strength to go with him. Thank you for the wisdom, faith, and strength to complete the task before me. Amen.

Friday night studying

Here I am again, Lord. It's Friday night and most of my friends are out partying and enjoying themselves.

While I'm not the only one in the library, I feel alone. You know how I question myself when I study too much.

SHARING THE LIGHT WITHIN THE VU COMMUNITY
Light for campus life
Faith and learning

Tonight there are new challenges. I commend each of them to you. Help me to stay focused. Steady. And when the evening is done, free me to let go. Enable me to relax and enjoy friends. Permit me the joy of savoring the completion of significant tasks. In Jesus' name. Amen.

Before an exam

Lord God,

You call, equip and test your servants that we may excel in your service. Be with me now as I face this exam.

Calm my racing mind. Ease my pounding heart.

You have commanded us to do all that we do in your name. Let the test that I now face be done to your glory, and may it strengthen me for your service. Amen.

Before another exam

God,

You have promised not to test us beyond what we are able. I hope you weren't kidding. Amen.

Prayer for my field of study

God of all knowledge,

There is so much to know and understand in your grand world. One way I am beginning to understand your creative and ordering presence is through my study of . . . . So many others have contributed to this field of study.

SHARING THE LIGHT WITHIN THE VU COMMUNITY
Light for campus life
Faith and learning

I am indebted to their diligence, rigor, and capacity to communicate their ideas to my generation.

Help me always to keep my passion for the study of . . . in perspective. Your world, your truth is so large, it is beyond one discipline's way of knowing and understanding.

I am grateful for others who share my interest in the field of . . . . May we, in our own ways, also be diligent, rigorous, and ever-willing to express our understanding of the basic ideas, concepts, and theories related to the field of . . . . Thank you for the privilege of learning about this fascinating aspect of your world. Amen.

Textbooks

Author and perfecter of all,

Every semester I purchase new books that are to lead me into greater understanding and application of various subjects. They contain the hard work of many people.

While I am grateful for the contributions of these authors, I have mixed feelings about the text that bears their name. Some are truly stimulating and worthy of close reading; others are dry, outdated, and hard to use. I wonder about the expense of some of these books, also.

Still, these are the texts I must master. Free me from attitudes that debilitate my study of and learning from these resources. Foster in me a spirit that uses course materials, however limited, to their and my full potential. Amen.

SHARING THE LIGHT WITHIN THE VU COMMUNITY
Light for campus life
Faith and learning

When studying Scripture

O God,

The ancient rabbis put it well: "Turn it and turn it again, for everything is in it." That is so true of the Scriptures. We come to them sure of ourselves, and they overwhelm us with mystery. We come in confusion, and they bring us clarity. We come in pain, and they bring us healing and joy. We come in guilt, and they convey your love and peace. We come in awe of you, and you show yourself vulnerable and acquainted with grief. We come ready to eat what scraps may fall, and you feast us with the Bread of Life. Grant us above all to see in these words the Word made flesh for our sakes. Amen.

Honor Code

God of all truth,

Over 60 years ago you led a band of VU students to create a code that established a way to behave when doing academic work. Thank you for giving them courage, foresight, and integrity.

Today I live in a different world where truth is more relative. People seek to operate by their own lights.

Some of my peers dismiss the code as outdated, often violated, and easily circumvented. When my moral compass wavers, and I am drawn to their thinking, steady my resolve to live by your light. Spare me the foolhardiness of shortcuts that provide temporary convenience. Stiffen my determination to do the work that leads to enduring knowledge.

Inspire me to be aware of those who over the past six decades followed the higher path of honesty and trustworthiness. In your spirit of truth and righteousness I depend and pray. Amen.

Prayer is . . .

. . . the conscious relating of everything seen and experienced to the presence of the living God in confident, heartfelt trust that the risen Christ gets revealed, indeed, whatever the situation.   – *Christoffer Grundmann*

. . . sitting, quietly
(breath in, breath out)
Listening, attentively
For the deep love of God.
– *Kristin Nygaard*

. . . my support throughout the day, my private conversations with God that occur anywhere and anytime.   – *Barb Lieske*

SHARING THE LIGHT WITHIN THE VU COMMUNITY
Light for campus life
Stress and struggle

Calmness

Gracious God,

Our days are cluttered with tasks and noise. We pray for your help in resisting the constant distractions of life in a 24/7 world. Lead us, we pray, beside still waters. Give us the strength to turn off the noise in order to share focused time with you. And, even then, when our bodies squirm and our minds wander, help us to receive our restlessness as a sign of our yearning to rest in you. We ask this in the name of the One who stilled the stormy sea, Jesus Christ our Lord. Amen.

In times of stress

God of peace,

I thank and praise you for each moment of life that you grant. When my days become chaotic, I often feel far from you and suffocated by my distorted sense of perspective.

Lord, your word has the power to calm raging waters. Trusting in that word, I pray that you would breathe into my weary and anxious bones these words of peace: "Be still and know that I am God."

Help me to remember that no matter what stressful situations I may encounter – you are Lord and I am your beloved child. Transform each moment of stress into an opportunity for me to use the gifts that you have given, and to reflect the joy that comes through your resurrection. Amen.

Transitioning to college

Dear Lord,

Transitioning to college has been hard. My family is far away and I don't know anyone. My courses have been difficult so far. Some

SHARING THE LIGHT WITHIN THE VU COMMUNITY
Light for campus life
Stress and struggle

I AM with you always,
to the end of the age.
Matthew 28:20

days I'm really overwhelmed with anxiety.
At times I feel paralyzed by fear. You are my hope
in such situations. Lord, please keep my mind
clear when I am making decisions. Give me the strength to work
hard and to overcome the fear of failing. Do not let apprehension
and doubt separate me from you. Amen.

For those suffering illness or injury

Dear God,

The amount of illness and injury in the world is overwhelming.
I find myself questioning you; why do you let this happen? Help
me to remember that you ARE above all a loving and gracious
God, and that you care for all your children, ill or well, injured or
healthy. Help me accept that I cannot always heal what is broken;
still, give me strength to do what I can to comfort and protect
those who are suffering. Work through me to accomplish what
I cannot do alone. Amen.

Homesickness

Ever-present God,

I am surprised that I feel so lost and homesick. I thought I had
made the transition.

These feelings are so distracting when I need to study. My friends
are weary of my talking about some place they've never been.
I know packing my bags and going home is no solution. I have
goals to realize, a scholarship to maintain, and the expectations
of significant others to meet.

Some days the longing to be home just sweeps me away. It's like
home is this big magnet drawing me back. Plus, it doesn't help
that my family misses me. How do I settle my heart when it longs
to be home?

SHARING THE LIGHT WITHIN THE VU COMMUNITY
  Light for campus life
  Stress and struggle

Ease my longing, Lord. Steady my jittery nerves. Renew my Valpo dreams. Keep me focused on today, and on the people and assignments that are here. Teach me how to overcome this challenge so that I might realize my potential in this place. Amen.

Course overload

Understanding God. . .

I think I've done it again. Why do I keep trying to do too much?

This semester it's a course overload. Even though taking extra credits can provide some new options next year, I am buckling under the additional pressure. My options are narrowing. The time is past for me to drop a course. A drop in my CGPA will jeopardize my academic goals.

I should have known better than to stretch myself like this. I'm feeling stuck with unpleasant options, Lord. Help me to take an honorable path, even if it means foregoing some other priorities this semester. Please God, see me through this quandary. Amen.

When I seem to have lost focus

Lord,

The demands in my life are many. Everything and everyone seems to want my immediate attention. I feel unfocused. I am second-guessing myself. I am neglecting my school work, my friends and, most importantly, you.

Help me to focus my life, Lord. Provide me with a sense of clarity regarding what is significant to do today, and instill in me the ability to stick with what is important for me to accomplish in the hours ahead. Amen.

SHARING THE LIGHT WITHIN THE VU COMMUNITY
Light for campus life
Stress and struggle

Disappointment

Heavenly Father,

Let me not be overcome with the disappointments of today nor fail to see all that you have given me. Rather, help me to seek out your good counsel and see your light. Steady me when things do not go as I expect, and be my shield when I am weak. Lift your servant when plans go awry, and guide me when I am disillusioned. Renewed by your grace, and strengthened by your Spirit, may I be inspired and empowered to do your will and proclaim your love. Amen.

Failure

Gracious and forgiving God,

You know our failures better than we ourselves. Come to us in our failings and weaknesses with your forgiving and loving presence. Teach us to see our failures in the light of your presence, so that we might forgive ourselves as you have already forgiven us. Help us to see, also, that our failures may be the occasion for you to call us to serve you, to live through our weakness, and to witness through our brokenness. Grant us the ability to trust you, that we might continue through our fears and failings to follow, in faith, in the One who brings us to new life. Amen.

Demanding Professor

Heavenly Father,

The stress is immense! The work load never ends and the papers are never good enough. Doesn't my professor realize that I have other classes and other commitments, not the least of which are my spiritual and emotional well-being?

I know you also demand much of me; when following you I also

SHARING THE LIGHT WITHIN THE VU COMMUNITY
Light for campus life
Stress and struggle

come up short. Still, I take comfort in the knowledge that all my failures have already been met by your son on that most harsh cross. His sacrifice gives me endurance and perspective as I strive to meet my teacher's expectations. Teach me to turn high expectations into opportunities to excel on this side of your eternal resting place. Amen.

When grades aren't what you expect

Lord,

What a jolt! My grades this semester did not turn out as I had hoped. Did I mess up or were my professors too unrealistic? Should I contest some of these grades? What's the message here?

Now that I think about it, this isn't the first time I have had my academic hopes dashed. Last time it happened I got mad and sulked and blamed others.

Spare me the same mistake, gracious God. Help me learn what I can do to improve the way my work is received. Keep me focused on being the best student I can be. In Jesus' name. Amen.

Transfer students

Gracious God,

Changing from one university to another is not as easy as I thought it would be. During this time of transition, infuse me with courage and optimism to begin a new and exciting chapter of my life. Provide me with faith to know and understand your will, and assurance that you will be with me and guide me each step of the way. Encourage me to embrace this change, and convince me that you have a plan and purpose for me and my life. Enable me to shine the light of your love wherever I go. In your name. Amen.

SHARING THE LIGHT WITHIN THE VU COMMUNITY
Light for campus life
Stress and struggle

When money is short

God of all provision. . .

Here I am again. What money I have left has to be set aside for basic expenses these next few weeks. That means I have no margin for error and no reserve for unexpected expenses and spontaneous fun stuff.

I feel like a pauper. My freedom to do what I want, when I want, is greatly curtailed.

What adds to my unease is my realization that I am healthy and able to study what interests me. I feel like an ungrateful person who is whining. Forgive me, gracious God, for my tendency to complain and lament my situation.

When money is short, like this, teach me to remember your many blessings, especially the gift of Jesus, my baptism, my life in this community of believers, and all the relationships with which you daily enrich my days. Amen.

Bad news from home

Lord of heaven and earth,

It's usually those around me who get jarring news from home. Now it's my turn.

You know my family and all our struggles. It seems like things have piled up at home. There are problems with my sibs. Dad's employment is uncertain. Mom's not been feeling well. Things are pretty tense around the house.

Here I am, away from home and facing my own set of challenges. Still, my heart aches for my family. I want to be there for them.

Help me sort through all of this bad news from home, Lord. Where I can make a difference, spur me to act. Where I can't impact things, teach me patience.

Dear Jesus, keep me praying on behalf of my family. Amen.

SHARING THE LIGHT WITHIN THE VU COMMUNITY
Light for campus life
Stress and struggle

Angry and frustrated

Merciful and gracious God,

Hear my cry.
Lord, I am so frustrated and upset.
My heart is pounding as anger surges within me.
I hate feeling this way...so furious and out of control.
In my exasperation, I cry out for your help.

O Lord, have mercy.

Remember me and walk with me during these
chaotic times.

Free me from the anger that threatens to overpower me.
And help me find ways of expressing my anger without lashing
out in bitterness and rage.

Fill me with your patience, O Lord, and guide me in your truth.
Forgive me, renew me, and help me to begin again.

For you are God, my Savior; and my hope is in you all day long.
Amen.

"
You must understand this, my beloved:
let everyone be quick to listen, slow to speak, slow to anger;
for your anger does not produce God's righteousness.

(James 1:19-20)
"

HARING THE LIGHT WITHIN THE VU COMMUNITY
Light for campus life
Stress and struggle

Courage to seek help

God of mercy and grace,

Things are not right in my life. I know it. My friends know it, too. Most days I have a sinking feeling that drains my energy.

What's complicating my life is that I'm afraid to admit what's happening to me. I keep denying that I need someone, a person who can hear me out and help me find a path back to the way I used to be.

Why is it so hard to own up to unproductive behaviors and attitudes? Or to check out if there is something medically wrong with me?

Lots of people once sought your son out for healing and hope. Help me to be one more who reaches out to Jesus and to those through whom he works today. I commend my frightened and weary spirit into your hands, dear God. Give me courage to reach out. Amen.

> "
> Lord, I do not ask that I never be afflicted,
> but only that you never abandon me in affliction.
>
> – *St. Bernadette of Lourdes (1844-1879)*
> "

SHARING THE LIGHT WITHIN THE VU COMMUNITY
  Light for campus life
  Stress and struggle
  Prayer is. . .

The dark night of the soul

Father God,

From the middle of our journey we cry out to you, weary and lost
Overcome by doubt, our work has drained us and our friends hav
fled. Gone is all comfort, and before us stretches a cold desert
of despair. You, Lord, seem distant, and we seem strangers. Reveal
again your son, Jesus Christ Emmanuel, tempted from below,
forsaken from above. Through him make use of this present
suffering in the gospel of our lives, and send your Spirit to mend
our hearts of all that breaks them. Amen.

Prayer is. . .

. . . listening to our hearts as we express
what we need, hope for, and hope against,
making our innermost desires plain to us,
even as God already knows them.
– *Margaret Franson*

. . . an ever-present opportunity to engage God
openly and honestly in an embrace
that deepens intimacy, trust, compassion and hope
while welcoming the reality of fears, anger,
doubts, confusion and disappointment.

– *David Simpson*

Life!

Lord of all life,

Sometimes I have to be reminded I AM ALIVE!
I have a life to live. A future that's open and promising.

So often I seem to be in glide mode where everything is taken
for granted. I lose touch with what it means to breathe deep and
smell, touch, taste, hear and see.

Granted, life is not smooth and simple. All of us who are marked
with the sign of the cross know of life's deep paradoxes: saint and
sinner, free and slave, death and resurrection.

May your Spirit:

- Stir me to honor and respect all of created life,
  not just my own.

- Stimulate me to love and defend all of created life,
  not just my own.

- Keep me mindful of, and thankful for, your daily gift
  of life.

- Strengthen my resolve to share my life with others
  for the sake of Jesus. Amen.

Freedom

Ever-freeing God…

Even if freedom is an overused word, thank you for keeping it
alive in your holy Word. How can I forget the way you freed your
people in Egypt so long ago? Or Jesus freeing so many who were
ill, possessed and lame?

Spare me shallow understandings of freedom, especially those that
are self-serving and destructive of others.

Shape in me a sense of freedom that takes me into the midst of my
neighbor's need. Center me in the great truth that those who lose

their lives for your sake will gain immeasurably more than envisioned.

Thank you for the freedom this day to study, to gather together with friends, to express my opinions. Most of all, thank you for the freedom to serve in the name of Jesus. Amen.

Praise for God's creation

"The heavens declare the glory of God."[1] With our modern telescopes, O Lord, we see today much farther than did the psalmist, to distant stars and galaxies.

You have made a wonderful universe, complex yet orderly. And you have given us intellects with which to study your handiwork.

"But what is man, that you are mindful of him?"[2] As our knowledge of the vastness of the universe increases, so does our awe at the thought that you are concerned about us, people on planet Earth, and that, in love, O holy God, you sent your son to save us from the just punishment for our sins.

May we live lives of thankfulness, loving you and our neighbors. May we care for your creation as good stewards and, as we gain in knowledge, may we glorify you all the more. Amen.

([1]Psalm 19:1 NIV; [2]Psalm 8:4)

Change in season

God of change. . . God of creation,

In the rushing winds and the pouring rains that engulf us,
in the subtle variations of the colors and textures of the trees,
in the cherished hours of sunlight and in the moonlit nights,
each day has its surprise for us. . .

Your hand has formed a beautiful creation that follows intricate patterns year after year, constantly shifting, always remarkable.

Through long hours of reading, talking, worrying, surrounded by life, we notice changes. We thank you for changes, for beauty, and for each day you light. Amen.

Joy

Lord,

Thank you for all the fruits of the Spirit you have given to me, especially joy. Even though I may not feel full of joy today, help me to be content. Remind me that joy is not being happy all the time, but it is knowing that you love me and that in you I can do anything. Just knowing that fills me with joy! Let your joy live in me in a way that blesses others. Amen.

Diversity

How could I ever have imagined, O God, that you were not great enough or good enough to grace the human race with the same variety and diversity so wonderfully visible in birds and trees and the whole created order. Yet part of me remains anxious and uncomfortable around people different from me. That's not what you intended. You intended us to be a blessing upon each other. Open me to receive the blessing others can bring me, especially in their being other than I am. And make me a blessing to them. Amen.   From *Valparaiso University Prayer Book*, 2001, p. 94

Ways to communicate

Lord,

I love to be understood. Endless are the ways of communicating meaning, intention and emotion. Ever-changing are the ways of communicating, whether by cell phones, internet, or face-to-face.

You have spoken to us through the prophets, through your son Jesus Christ, and through the movement of your Holy Spirit. Help us to hear your spirit today through all the varied ways we have of communicating.

Let me be continually grateful for those who seek to broaden and strengthen the avenues of communication. Help me to not take for granted the many ways to communicate nor misuse them for ill-conceived results.

I pray all in the name of him who seeks to communicate with all as they have ears to hear and eyes to see. Amen.

Student Senate

Lord of power and might, Lord of compassion and love,

I bring before you the Student Senate, its members and advisors. Thank you for each of them, their energy, dedication, and insight.

As they seek your will for the student body and this university, I humbly ask that all catch a vision of, and subsequently experience, what it means to be servant leaders in the likeness of your son. Please help students and advisors alike to exercise their power wisely and in a compassionate manner; temper their zeal with reflection before making decisions.

May they be good stewards of the resources you have provided for their use; guide them to honor you by allocating these resources to others in a manner that enables your kingdom to be realized on our campus. Amen.

RA and floor-mates

Living God,

Here I am. Paired with a roommate. Part of a floor of fellow students. Guided by an RA I hardly know.

What will come of this arrangement? How will things work out, especially with some of the new people down the hall?

Draw out the best in me this year, Lord. Keep me from centering only on my friends and ignoring those I do not know well. Grant me a spirit of thankfulness for those on my floor this year.

Teach me to be sensitive to others, willing to hear their concerns, open to being admonished for ill-conceived actions, and ready to lend a hand when needed.

Stir me to lift up rather than put down, to voice hope rather than pessimism, and to help build a responsive spirit on the floor. Amen.

A prayer for housekeepers

They remind me of you, Lord God, as they sweep away the dirt from the floor, dust the shelves, wipe down the walls and haul out the trash. Often unnoticed, the housekeeper dutifully cleans our place just like you. You, Lord, dust me off, wipe me down and sweep out the dirt of my life, removing the trash that soils me through my sin-bearer Jesus. I am grateful for your cleansing love. I am grateful for our faithful housekeepers. Notice them, Lord, and bless them in the name of Jesus. Amen.

Music in my life

Make a joyful noise unto the Lord!

With grateful praise I thank you for your blessing of music. For the warmth, joy, and hope it brings to others, let me be your instrument.

Make a joyful noise unto the Lord!

Help me to empower, strengthen, and uplift others with the gift of music. By teaching, playing, and singing, let me inspire others to praise you. May your love shine through to all people.

Make a joyful noise unto the Lord! Amen.

Birthday

O God of endless possibilities,

I am humbled that out of all that might have been, you have chosen to create me, granting me a BIRTH day. You have also given me the greater gift of life in Christ through the waters of Holy Baptism. Forgive my indiscretions, inadequacies, and intolerance of others and help me to lead a life well-lived in harmony with your will. As I celebrate my birthday, make me mindful of the blessed opportunity to live a life of service to you and others. Help me to share that blessing with everyone I meet. I ask this in Jesus' name. Amen.

Special recognition

Giver of all good gifts. . .

To be recognized by others is really astounding! It's like frosting on the cake or an unexpected "A" on an exam. Do I deserve this recognition? Part of me says, "Of course. I've worked hard. I really have done something worthy of praise."

But there is another voice that says, "Others have contributed to my success. Others have sharpened my thinking, stimulated me to push ahead, and challenged me to excel."

At the end of the day, there are many others who could also be recognized. And for reasons you alone may know, I'm the one to be lauded this time.

All thanks and glory be to you who sustains, redeems, and renews me. Keep me humble and eager to contribute to others' success as well, precious God. Amen.

Music in the Chapel

Jesus Christ, joy of all,

We give you thanks for the music that fills the Chapel of the Resurrection. May we use this gift to praise the one who has ended the night of sin in our hearts.

Just as we are one in the body of Christ, may our united voices glorify you, our savior and our redeemer. Lord, we also ask that the music not distract us from the true purpose of worship, but rather that it serve to draw our hearts closer to you. May the strength you give to our voices make the powers of darkness know that they have no place in our hearts as you live in us, now and forever. Amen.

Renewed energy

Lord God,

Some days I feel so exhausted, completely drained of energy. At times such as these, I remember Ezekiel, who felt so beleaguered that he longed to be with you. If it is not my time to join you (and I hope it isn't!), guide me to your refreshing waters. Re-energize me that I may glorify you with a renewed spirit. Help me keep in check that which saps my energy and turn my focus on you in my day-to-day life.

May my renewed energy flow toward others in loving ways. Amen.

Nighttime prayer

Heavenly Father,

Take my burdens from me as I sleep. Keep me from hanging on to that which destroys and distracts. Let me rest in your promise of forgiveness.

Watch over my family and friends as they sleep. Grant them peace and hope. Protect them throughout this night. Help them grow closer to you.

I pray for all those who don't have a bed tonight, and for those who may be sleeping outside. Lord, console and protect them. Help them know that you are with them.

I pray your peace may make its way throughout the world tonight. Purify all hearts of violence and hardness, and let us rest securely in your Son, Jesus Christ. Amen.

This amazing day

Thank you for this amazing day, Lord.

For friends and families and strangers.
Thank you for this amazing day, Lord.

For birds, fish, and bees.
Thank you for this amazing day, Lord.

For trees, flowers, and thorns.
Thank you for this amazing day, Lord.

For happiness, humor, and laughter.
Thank you for this amazing day, Lord.

For your life, love, and resurrection.
Thank you for being so amazing, Lord.

For everything you have given your creation.
Thank you for being so amazing, Lord.

Amen.

Graduates of Valpo

Lord,

Most of those who have graduated from Valpo are unknown to me. Others I know only through yearbooks, student newspapers, plaques, and stories that get told.

Still, I feel a kinship. A connection. A bond based upon a dream, a common purpose, an honor code, shared facilities, and learning from or being in class with some of the same teachers.

While I may meet only a select number of VU graduates, I am grateful for their contributions to this place. Thank you for imbuing so many of them with a sense of integrity, competence, and faith. Their successes continue to pave the way for those of us soon to graduate.

May we, too, be prepared to make our contributions, whether in business, the arts, athletics, teaching, engineering, medicine, communications, social work, nursing, law, the church or wherever our vocation leads us. Amen.

Grateful for our founders' vision

Heavenly Father,

We come to you with gratitude and praise for the men and women who created and shaped our University through generations past. Their collective talent, wisdom, perseverance, and voices have placed in our hands a special place where faith and learning flourish as twin ideals and twin realities.

We are indebted to our founders and to all who have, and still, steward the resources of this University. Humbly and joyously, we pray for the wisdom, talent, and courage to exceed our founders' greatest hopes and dreams, and to bestow this great University with everything it needs to serve countless generations to come. We ask this in the name of your Son. Amen.

Growing in wisdom, stature, and favor

Father of Jesus,

The Scriptures describe how your beloved son grew in wisdom, stature, and favor with you and all people. Jesus seemed so committed to learning, so healthy, so interested in others.

Thank you for instilling in me a hunger to grow in wisdom. I am grateful that my mind is permeable. Inspire me to be an ardent student.

Thank you for providing me a body that follows its innate capacity to grow. I am grateful to be so hearty. Challenge me to eat, sleep, and exercise well.

Thank you for a relationship with you that keeps me grounded and purposeful. I am grateful that you claimed and named me in my baptism. Hold me close, dear Father.

Thank you for the many rich and uplifting relationships that fill my life. I am grateful that I catch a glimpse of your love through others. Lead me to serve as I have been served.

Keep me growing, God, please. Amen.

> **In the beginning we are indeed the subject and the center of our prayers. But in God's time and in God's way a Copernican revolution takes place in our heart. Slowly, almost imperceptibly, there is a shift in our center of gravity. We pass from thinking of God as part of our life to the realization that we are part of his life.**
>
> – *Richard Foster, writer, theologian*

SHARING THE LIGHT WITHIN THE VU COMMUNITY
Light for campus life
Sorrow and loss

So sudden

Healing God,

Out of the blue! The call came so normally. But the message took my breath away: Leukemia… I can barely say the word, much less grasp the illness.

Why does this kind of sickness take over a person? What I do know is this: I'm stunned, scared, full of questions. I want answers. I need help.

For now, Lord, steady me so I can think clearly, listen well and respond sensitively. Later, I will pray for a better diagnosis and for a sparing restoration. Be with me, Jesus, as I pray in your name. Amen.

Time of pain

God of all that is, was, and will be,

You are my maker. I owe you my life.

Yet the life I live is full of pain. I feel like Job of yesteryear, who lost all and lived in cascading bouts of mental, physical and eternal anguish. *Humbly, I ask for your relief, O God of mercy.*

You know all, O Lord. Is my pain only of my own mind and hand's doing? If so, like Job, guide me to confess my contributions to my calamities. *Patiently, I seek your relief, O Lord of healing.*

Spare me the bitterness and resentment that comes from asking, "Why me, God?" Keep me also from resignation and despair that leads to the miry pit. *Hopefully, I pray my pleas will bring your relief, O Lord of life.*

Like Job, lead me to say, "I know that you can do all things, and that no purpose of yours can be thwarted."[1] *Faithfully, I trust in your mercy and healing, O God of promise.* ([1]Job 42:2)

SHARING THE LIGHT WITHIN THE VU COMMUNITY
Light for campus life
Sorrow and loss

Into your hands I commend myself, Lord. Supply whatever healing you wish; if not healing, courage to face the day, content in your grace and mercy. In Jesus' name. Amen

Deep sorrow

Heavenly Father,

In this dark time, how do I carry on?
Emotionally, physically, I hurt.
I am blinded by grief.

Exhausted, I open my heart to your light. You are with me, and always have been. I trust in your guidance as the healing process unfolds.

I am grateful for the solace you provide me.
Family, friends, even strangers support me.
Tears, and at times laughter, flow with deep release.

I do not know the larger picture – you do.
With trust in you I carry on, knowing that everything is – and will be – as it should be. Amen.

A death

Lord,

Gone are the opportunities to talk, to dream, to share in the fullness of life. Death robs us again. My head tells me to remember St. Paul's triumphant words in Romans 8:38-39:

For I am convinced that neither death, nor life, nor angels, nor rulers, nor things present, nor things to come, nor powers, nor height, nor depth, nor anything else in all creation, will be able to separate us from the love of God in Christ Jesus our Lord.

SHARING THE LIGHT WITHIN THE VU COMMUNITY
  Light for campus life
  Sorrow and loss

My heart tells me a different story. I feel an emptiness, an ache, an abiding loss. In your original creation, God, all was well. No death, only life. Not today. How sad that we must taste, again and again, the fruits of a fallen world.

Remind me that any distress once experienced is now alleviated. Settle any lingering bitterness or doubt with the assurance that Jesus Christ overcame death and brings life and immortality through his resurrection. Lift my spirit with the promise that the one I have lost is now in your arms. Amen.

For those who mourn

Loving and understanding God,

I pray for you to be with me now in this time of confusion and grief.

I know that you provide, Lord, and that you do not abandon your fold, but I do feel at a loss; I do feel abandoned.

I ask for your help, that I might find rest and assurance in you as I grieve.

But not just I, Lord –

Be with all those who mourn the loss of one of your precious servants. There are family and friends, too, who grieve, and they need help also.

Be present. Help me be a vessel, no longer broken but whole, that carries your comforting word to those who hurt and offers your strength to those who feel overcome. Thank you for healing me so I might heal others. In your holy name, dear God. Amen.

SHARING THE LIGHT WITHIN THE VU COMMUNITY
Light for campus life
Leaving or returning to campus

Before a trip taken together

Almighty God,

Wherever we go, whenever we get there, you are already there ahead of us. However we travel, whatever the road, you pace the way beside us.

Where can we go from your Spirit? If we ascend to heaven, you are there. If we lie down in Sheol, you are there.

If we take the wings of the morning and dwell in the uttermost parts of the sea, even there your hand shall lead us, and your right hand shall hold us. (Psalm 139:7-10)

Go with us now.

Keep us safe from danger as we go.

Grant us confidence when we arrive.

We trust, O Lord, in your steadfast faithfulness, for you yourself have promised us: "Mountains may depart and the hills be removed, but my steadfast love shall not depart from you." (Isaiah 54:10)

So be it with us now. Amen.

Out for a good time

Lord,

Some of my friends think Christians can never have a good time because those friends can't imagine real fun without reckless behavior and drinking to excess. Even I wonder sometimes if faithful living is merely self-denial and sacrifice.

Jesus, your word made flesh, has taught a different way. He loved a good time – enjoying good food with friends, telling stories, relaxing, and, of course, he did once turn all that water into wine. But he never used food or drink, nor did he tell stories, except in a way that gave you glory and left his friends grateful.

SHARING THE LIGHT WITHIN THE VU COMMUNITY
Light for campus life
Leaving or returning to campus

After a hard week of studies, I'm really looking
forward to this weekend, Lord, and I want that
kind of good time. Help me to live out Jesus' way,
wherever I am and whomever I'm with, so that I may give
witness to a love of life and a joyous celebration that hurts no one,
including me, and leaves both me and others thanking you.
In Jesus' name. Amen.

Going on a servant event

Jesus, servant of humankind,

You have been with us through our planning. Be with us now as
we begin our servant event.

Thank you for this opportunity to serve you in a new setting.
Instill a servant spirit in our group. Keep us from behavior that
condescends or misrepresents you. Help us understand and respect
those whom we serve.

If a mishap befalls us, provide us courage and support. Lift our
spirits to be caring and sensitive with one another. Forgive us if we
seem nervous and untrusting.

May your angels accompany us as we travel. Provide our drivers a
special measure of alertness. Use us to show the love of Christ to
others. Teach us through this venture, O Lord. Amen.

Touring with a musical group

God of all sound and harmony,

We're almost ready for this trip – that is, the music is almost
learned and the transportation logistics are in place. Our program
is beautiful, and it makes us proud to be part of a group that can
present such a wonderful concert. Keep us safe on the road, Lord,
and give us the good spirits to get along with each other, even

SHARING THE LIGHT WITHIN THE VU COMMUNITY
Light for campus life
Leaving or returning to campus

though there are bound to be glitches along the way. Let us remember that our gifts come from you, even those that we've spent long hours improving, and so inspire us to make music as a way to glorify you and uplift those who attend our concerts. Amen.

Adapted from *Valparaiso University Prayer Book*, 2001, p. 131

Heading home for a break

Good and gracious Lord,

Whoever designed the academic calendar deserves a pat on the back. Breaks seem to come just in time. That's another way of saying I'm really weary of studying. My interest in classes seems to be stalled at this point, and the last round of exams were so much wasted effort. I'm disappointed in myself.

I need to have my energy restored, and maybe being at home will do that. If I start to get impatient when little things aggravate me about my family, keep my focus on all the good things at home. Turn my attention to ways that regenerate and enable me to contribute to the well-being of my family.

If it be your will, bring me back to school with renewed excitement about what's left to do this semester. Amen.

> **When we close our eyes to the deep needs of other people whether they live on the streets or under our own roof – and when we close our eyes to our own deep need to reach out to them – we can never be fully at home anywhere.**
>
> *– Frederick Buechner, minister, author (1926-   )*

SHARING THE LIGHT WITHIN THE VU COMMUNITY
  Light for campus life
  Leaving or returning to campus

Students abroad

Dear Father,

I feel so blessed that I am able to study abroad.

I praise you for the opportunity to meet new people and explore new places.

Diverse languages, fresh food, colorful clothing, fascinating customs… I am learning and growing so much.

Rolling meadows, glassy water, open sky, bright warm sun… I am awestruck by the beauty of your creation.

Sometimes, though, overseas travel is stressful and hazardous. Thank you for keeping me safe throughout this journey.

Sometimes I also feel lonely and far from home. Thank you for giving me friends throughout this journey.

I am so glad you are my rock.

I am so grateful you are my shepherd. Amen.

Feeling cut off from friends

Heavenly Father,

Time and distance can cause havoc with the best of relationships. Right now, I'm feeling pretty cut off from my friends.

In this age of instant communication, it's astounding that I feel this way. Maybe I just miss the great face-to-face conversations we used to have.

Keep me mindful during these times that, though I am far from those I love, I am close to them through you and your ever-loving son. Thank you for the memories of good times and the little reminders that they are thinking of me. Help me return to them safely. In your blessed name. Amen.

SHARING THE LIGHT WITHIN THE VU COMMUNITY
Light for campus life
Leaving or returning to campus

Returning from off-campus studies

Dear Father,

You are everywhere and know everything. You know that life is full of uncertainty and change. As I return from my time away from campus, remind me that you are the only constant in my life. While relationships have changed, other people have changed, and certainly I have changed, you remain the same. When things seem uncertain and I feel like a stranger on campus, help me to rely on your unchanging love as my foundation. Keep alive what I have learned and let it enrich all with whom I now relate. Amen.

Finding a summer job

With all I have to attend to over the next weeks, God, I am really feeling pressed. The last thing I need to be doing is worrying about finding a summer job. But I am.

I know summer jobs don't just happen. So far all my efforts have come to naught.

Hear the ill-expressed cries of my heart (decent money, change of pace, nice location, stimulating experience) and open the doors that you want me to walk through. I'll do my part filling out applications and following up. Thank you for listening and understanding, gracious God. Amen.

Adapted from *Valparaiso University Prayer Book*, 2001, p. 170

> **"** *For surely I know the plans I have for you,
> says the LORD, plans for your welfare and not for harm,
> to give you a future with hope. Then when you call
> upon me and come to pray to me, I will hear you.*
>
> *(Jeremiah 29:11-12)* **"**

To know God

Dear God,

Some days I feel as though I don't know you.

Some days I feel as though I don't want to know you.

Abide with me, Lord, and grant me *patience*.

You knew me before I knew myself;

You have given me my very life by your love.

I pray you bestow unto me both the desire and the ability to see your presence today, from the dawn's first rays until I lay my head to rest at night. Help me to draw nearer to you, that I may experience your infinite love with open arms and a willing heart. Amen.

For parents

Nurturing God,

I realize how fortunate I am, especially to have a mother and father who love me and want the best for me. Thank you for motivating my parents to provide a safe and loving setting in which to mature. Imbue me with a gratitude that nurtures our relationship.

Help my parents live in ways that honor you. As they face challenges at work, church, and in the neighborhood, provide them with wisdom and hope.

Please be present with all those who have experienced homes sundered by divorce, death or other difficulties. Where scars or present hurts remain, bring forth your healing and hope.

Keep me attuned to ways I can honor my parents and confirm the abiding appreciation and respect I have for them, even when they make decisions that cause me concern. Amen.

A parent's prayer

Good and gracious God,

The time is here. My children are getting ready to go to college and be "on their own." Just yesterday it seems I was putting them on the bus for elementary school.

I can't wait for them to uncover their calling, to discover new and unique aspects of themselves, and to tap into hidden passions for learning and life. Confirm for them, Lord, the gifts you have given them.

I ask that you continue to guide me as a parent so I can be loving and supportive, courageous and strong, firm and objective in situations that are not easy for them or me.

Continue to bless our family, heavenly Father, so that in all we do we may be a blessing to others, sharing the abundance you have given us. Amen.

A roommate's prayer

Dear Father,

Thank you so much for my roommate and the opportunity to deepen our relationship. Please help me recognize and appreciate our various strengths and gifts even through difficult times.

When confronted by difficult times or differences of opinion, teach us patience and understanding. Let the Scripture directive be our guide to *bear with one another in love, making every effort to maintain the unity of the Spirit in the bond of peace.* (Ephesians 4:2b-3) When either of us is overtaken by fatigue, worry or hardship, restore us with your peace and presence. Grant harmony to our room, that it may be a safe place and a haven from daily pressures. Help us be and do our best this day. Amen.

For friends

Jesus, friend of all,

You have placed meaningful relationships in my life throughout the years. I am blessed to have a community of friends that surround me. Thank you for their positive impact on my life.

Keep me and my friends humble and open to the needs of each other. May we continue to grow deeper in our friendship and appreciation of our journey together.

God, your faithfulness is evident. I pray that I will emulate you by being a loyal friend in word and deed, and so continue to honor you through these relationships. Amen.

Balancing my loves

Lord of life,

I love to be with my friends. I also love to take on challenging tasks, coursework included. Sometimes I lose my balance. I dive into homework and ignore my buddies. Other times I'm all about relationships and ignore my classroom responsibilities.

I feel like a mobile that's easily out of kilter. Help me strike a balance that does justice to tasks and relationships. When I go off the deep end, and my academics or my friends suffer from a lack of attention, remind me of who and what needs my energy. Live in my heart and mind in a way that keeps my loves kindled, yet in perspective. In Jesus' name. Amen.

When feeling rejected

Oh Lord,

Rejection stings. It also corrodes one's spirit, burrowing deep inside.

Why does it keep happening to me? Am I that unworthy? Difficult to be around? Or am I overreacting and imposing myself on others?

It's one thing to apply to be an RA and not be selected. It's another thing to have people I know spurn me.

Oh Lord, you know the sting of rejection. You alone can halt the corrosion of my spirit. Please send me the comforter, your Holy Spirit, who can reverse the damage to my heart, mind and soul. Somehow, turn my experience of rejection into something positive. I trust you to help me do so. Amen.

When betrayed by someone

Maybe it was "not on purpose," but I still hurt. I thought we were friends. Now I feel betrayed and empty.

God, grant me the grace to live through this. I need to find a way to talk about my feelings without causing more pain.

You who know much about being wounded by others, help me – help us – listen to each other so we can restore our fragile relationship. Stretch my heart – stretch both of our hearts – so that your understanding and love fill us.

If I can forgive, and my friend cannot, let it be enough for me. Keep me mindful that I am not walking this journey alone. You are always with me. Amen.

Forgiving others

Forgive us our sins as we forgive those who sin against us…

I say these words so easily, Lord.
Why is the doing so impossibly hard?

Forgive as you have been forgiven…

I don't want to, Lord.
I want to hold onto the anger, rehearse the wounding words, polish my precious position.
I don't think I want this relationship that hurts so much.

Father, forgive them…

I do want a relationship with you, though.
You have already redeemed these circumstances.
Help me get out of the way of your grace.
Teach me to cherish a forgiving heart.
In Jesus' name. Amen.

Healing of relationships

Dear Lord,

There are people who have hurt me, and whom I have hurt in return. How easily and tragically it happened.

Please give me the strength to forgive them completely, as you have so often forgiven me. Grant me also the courage and humility to apologize and ask forgiveness wherever it is needed. Help me to realize that every person, no matter how irritable or hurtful at times, is one of your precious creations. May your healing power allow these relationships to be restored to a deeper and more profound level.

Help me to keep you always at the center of my relationships with others, and aid me in treating others in ways that honor you. In your name I ask this all. Amen.

My place in this group

Lord,

This is a group that deserves my wholehearted participation. The reason it gathers is a laudable one. But what's my role? Do I step up and lead? Or do I lay back and follow? What's my place in this group?

This much I know. The gifts you have given me can be used by this group. Guide me on how best, and when, to make my contribution. Thanks for groups that have a purpose, Lord. Keep me flexible and willing to do what's needed for the common good. Amen.

How shall I love my enemy?

Heavenly Father,

How shall I love my enemy? Can I love someone who would destroy what I love? Your answer, O Lord: *Let this mind be in you which was also in Christ Jesus… [who] became obedient to the point of death, even the death of the cross.* (Philippians 2:5, 8 NKJV)

Can we love as Christ loved? Is not the Church's history a testimony to our failure to forgive as we are forgiven and our willingness to inflict suffering rather than suffer?

Yet, when our failures meet your eternal patience and pity, we begin to see that we are neither who we think we are nor what we can be. Send us, therefore, the spirit of Jesus to make us instruments of your eternal patience and pity, so that our enemies might also see themselves not as they are but as they can be in your grace. This we pray in the name of our Prince of Peace, Jesus Christ. Amen.

Preparing for a date

God, my maker,

You created me to find joy in human society and in my relationships with others. Bless me now as I prepare for this date. Fill me with confidence in your faithfulness, that I may present myself with honesty and integrity.

Guide me with your wisdom that I treat my date with respect. Fill us with your Spirit that we may find delight in each other's company. In all that we say and do, may we be a witness to your generous grace. In the name of Jesus. Amen.

At the end of a relationship

Saving God,

In this moment, I am desperate and completely in need of your redeeming grace. Bring a resurrection out of this relationship's death.

I am broken. My emotions are inconsistent and uncontrollable. Allow me to surrender all of it to you. Hold me close.

Bring both of us, our families, and friends to a place of peace where the pain of this ending can no longer taint our actions toward one another. Keep me from impatience and accusation. Each day, help me let go of resentment and regret, and let your love in me overcome all these thoughts. Transform me, saving God. Amen.

About a serious relationship

Gentle, loving God,

Thank you for creating us to be in meaningful relationships with those around us. Thank you, especially, for the joy that comes from getting to know another deeply.

You have watched our relationship unfold. You know the hopes and dreams that live in our growing affection. Free us from the self-absorption of the moment and teach us how to maintain appropriate boundaries. Spare us a possessive spirit, and lead us to respectful interdependence.

As we grow in our relationship, may we responsibly live the lives to which you have called us and may our relationship strengthen us to accomplish your purpose. In your Son's holy name we pray. Amen.

Engagement

Loving God,

You created love, and now have blessed us with the gift of each other. ***Thank you for the joy and blessing of engagement.***

Surround us with your love as we prepare for marriage.
May the decisions and plans we now make glorify you.

Guide us through the transitions with family and friends as we make a commitment to each other. ***Thank you for the love made perfect in your Son, who fills our relationship with grace and forgiveness.***

May we continue to grow in love for you and each other.
In Jesus' name we pray. Amen.

Greek life

Gracious God,

You have blessed those of us in fraternities and sororities with a marvelous opportunity to pursue a singular purpose, engage in common endeavors, and forge deep and lasting friendships. However, often our desire for a strong brotherhood or sisterhood comes at the expense of so many of our brothers and sisters.

Just as we are called to reconcile first with those around us (Matthew 5:24), help us to heal the rivalries of our own creation so that we can spread the one true, fraternal love which is shown to us through the sacrifice of your Son, a love which transcends any single affiliation. We pray this through Christ our Lord. Amen.

When confronted with gossip

Dear Jesus,

Gossip, gossip, gossip . . . How easy it is to follow the crowd and talk about others behind their backs. Whether true or not, how easy it is to pass on the latest word about others. Sometimes my circle is abuzz with half-truths about people we know well or hardly at all.

Help me remember that those I talk about are also your children. Please forgive me for repeating malicious stories about others. Guide me to look into my own heart before I start degrading others.

When you dwell in my heart, I rest secure and am able to resist the subtle temptations to gossip. Lead me and my friends to protect the reputation of others so that we, and they, may spend our time in more worthy pursuits. I ask this in your holy name. Amen.

Prayer is. . .

. . . a cell phone from heaven.
A direct line, freely given without a charge.
God never screens our calls or puts us on hold.
God lovingly answers every call. – *Rin Seibert*

. . . the peaceful joy that is experienced between
you and the Lord. It is the most fulfilling part of my day.

– *Jane Claiborne*

SHARING THE LIGHT WITHIN THE VU COMMUNITY
Light for campus life
Being a light

Attentiveness

Heavenly Father,
>   You have brought us waking
>   to another new moment
>   in this world.

Make us mindful of all the life and beauty
>   that adorn the world you created;
>   and help us attend to it.

Make us mindful of this world
>   and Jesus' reconciling life and death;
>   and help us attend to him.

Make us mindful of all the hurt and suffering
>   that afflict the world you created;
>   and help us attend to it.

May we be attentive to you and your creation,
>   until you close our eyes at last
>   and in the name of Jesus call us home.
>   Amen.

Jesus in my everyday life

Jesus Christ,

You came into the world unknown, lived in the world misunderstood, and died in the world unaccepted.

You lived bravely; please give me courage to follow you daily. You died willingly; please give me perseverance to obey you daily.

Let me be to the world as you eternally are: a light in the darkness. Let me emulate you in guiding those who are lost and lifting up those who have fallen. Help me live in the world unashamed and let me die in this world rejoicing. Amen.

SHARING THE LIGHT WITHIN THE VU COMMUNITY
Light for campus life
Being a light

The nine fruits of the Spirit

I believe your promise, Lord. If I live in my
natural way the results will not be pretty. Your word speaks of ugly
and treacherous behaviors. (Galatians 5:16-21)

Rather, I seek to live another of your other promises: *But the
fruit of the Spirit is love, joy, peace, patience, kindness, goodness,
faithfulness, gentleness and self-control. Against such things there
is no law.* (Galatians 5:22-23 NIV)

I know that these gifts of your Spirit are what you desire for me.
Teach me to live them out in ways that glorify you and enhance
my classmates, family, teachers, and all who cross my path. Amen.

Courage

Jesus,

You understand courage so well. You also know how courage
can leave a person. You witnessed your disciples shrink from
you in your time of trial and tribulation. You also experienced
the courage of the woman who showered you with an ointment
of affection and respect.

There are times you infuse me with courage, Lord. I am able to
speak boldly of my love for you, take on new challenges, stand
up for the weak and dispossessed. But then I can also be paralyzed
by fear. Today is a bit like that. I don't think I can be brave for you
or anyone else. Not on my own.

Teach me to find my courage in you alone. And, Lord, let the
courage that you give me come out in words and actions of love.
Amen.

SHARING THE LIGHT WITHIN THE VU COMMUNITY
Light for campus life
Being a light

Self-image

Heavenly Father,

I, a sinful being, come to you asking that you help me see myself as the special and beautiful person you created. In your abounding love, you have shaped me in my mother's womb, unique in all creation.

You, heavenly Father, have declared that I am precious in your sight. You have called me by name to be your child through baptism. You continue to show me your forgiveness and mercy through the Gospel and Lord's Supper.

Daily create in me a clean heart that is able to remember and claim your promises. May all whom I encounter know that they, too, are shaped in your image. In the name of the Father, the Son, and the Holy Spirit. Amen.

For modesty

To my Father who loves me, and to Jesus to whom I am beautiful, I lift up my heart to you, O Lord.

Keep me, my King, from exposing my heart and my soul in ways which dishonor the beauty you see within me.

You wrote, my Bridegroom, of the beauty in me that so captivates your heart and expresses your glory.

The crown of creation, pure holiness I crave –
To be holy in my actions and honoring to my King.

I ask for wisdom, my Lord, to never with my body unleash a level of intimacy that could cause my brother to stumble.

Lord, help me to cherish my body as you cherish my soul:
In purity and humility, and in captivating radiance.

I love you, my Lord.
Give me wisdom, my King.
I cherish you, Jesus, for you find me captivating. Amen.

SHARING THE LIGHT WITHIN THE VU COMMUNITY
Light for campus life
Being a light

Expressions of intimacy

Lord God of all creation,

You invite us to share in your love,
to love our neighbors,
and to love ourselves.

You made us both body and soul
for love, bestowing upon us our sexuality,
the gift to one day cleave to another,
to become one flesh,
in the loving embrace of unity.

Yet, I often find myself struggling
with worldly torments,
when lust invades my heart,
attempting to replace my innermost
desire for true love,
love that sacrifices rather than conquers.

May you strengthen me and guide me,
O Loving God,
that in my intimacy with another
you may abide,
and your love be brought to perfection
in us. Amen.

Purify and transform our stained hearts

Lord Jesus,

Forgive us for becoming too busy – with hearts cluttered and soiled
by the demands and desires of this world – to see you each day, in
your word, in your creation, and in your blessings. Whether in the
feverish treadmill of our lives or in the precious, quiet moments,
calm and restore our hurried spirits, settle and renew our busy
minds, purify and transform our stained hearts so that we might
focus our entire being on you, your great wisdom, your nurturing
presence, and your perfect love. In your precious name. Amen.

SHARING THE LIGHT WITHIN THE VU COMMUNITY
Light for campus life
Being a light

Service

Christ Jesus,

Show me the road of justice and peace
and walk beside me along the way.

Make me humble
in a world that rewards the proud.

Give me patience
in a world that esteems the ambitious.

Open my heart
to a world crying out to be heard.

Shape my mind like yours
so that, like you,
I will empty myself of self.

Then,
fill me with the desire to serve
you,
your word,
and your people. Amen.

Before competition

Dear God,

I am grateful for the opportunity to grow and excel in competition. Thank you for the chance to complete the work that has led up to this event. Keep me safe today, and guard me against my pride so that I do not lose sight of you. Help me remember to compete to glorify you and not to gain glory from others. May I seek your will and not my own. As I go forth today, bless me with your strength and your love so I may show that strength and love to others. Amen.

SHARING THE LIGHT WITHIN THE VU COMMUNITY
Light for campus life
Being a light

When the party begins

Lord,

Lots of my friends have been getting ready for this party.
It promises to be a cool time.

Like other times, I seek your guiding hand. You have helped me
walk the fine line between loosening up and letting it all hang out.

I wish to honor you in all I do. I also seek to be a good friend who
can have a good time and affirm others' need to do so.

Keep me mindful of my values, Lord. Align my behavior with
what I believe. Help me affirm lighthearted humor, playful
interactions, good-intentioned socializing. If the party gets out
of control, help me be a part of the solution rather than part
of the problem. Be present, Lord. Amen.

Moderation

God our maker,

You, who have created the time for work and the Sabbath for rest,
teach us to balance our capacity for creating with our capacity for
being replenished.

You, who have created a fruitful earth and a people in need, teach
us to balance our individual and communal identities.

You, whose Spirit is the air we breathe in, the air we breathe out,
teach us to balance what we receive with what we give.

You, who have created all good things, teach us always to enjoy
them in generous moderation.

In your good time, we pray. Amen.

SHARING THE LIGHT WITHIN THE VU COMMUNITY
Light for campus life
Being a light

Sticking with God-pleasing priorities

Dear Father,

I pray that you will join all components of my life and be the guiding light to my priorities. Too often, I put first that which is frivolous, despite my heart's desire for you. Forgive me for the self-centeredness of my priorities.

Allow me to distinguish what is important from what is detrimental to my walk with you. Help me in each moment to keep my gaze upon you so that my priorities will reflect your will.

With the assurance of your steadfast grace, I place my life, all my plans and efforts, more fully into your hands. Amen.

Keeping fit

Lord,

Keeping fit seems like a pretty simple matter. Eat right, get sufficient sleep, exercise regularly, stay connected to you. I know the routine.

Yet, Lord, there always seems to be a "yet." I overeat; I need to pull an all-nighter; bad weather messes up my exercise program; I get distracted and ignore you.

I realize my body is your temple. I know you want me to be fit enough to reflect your love.

Guide me to do my part. Lead me to place my worries in your hands. Stir me to make healthy decisions. Keep me from being overly compulsive about being fit. I praise you for the mind, body, and spirit you have given me. I thank you for renewing me daily to be all I can be. Amen.

SHARING THE LIGHT WITHIN THE VU COMMUNITY
Light for campus life
Being a light

For strength in temptation

Dear God,

I come to you seeking strength in the vulnerable areas of my life where temptation is ever lurking. I pray that you would be with me in these trying times, and keep me from battling on my own.

Examine my heart and empty me of my evil ways. Cleanse my soul and fill me with desires that seek only you. Grant me the courage to draw away from those things and individuals that tempt me to sin. Teach me to surround myself with situations that edify your majesty and with people who glorify your holy name. In Jesus I pray. Amen.

Giving and receiving

Why is there that moment of awkwardness, God, when giving or receiving a gift? Is there, perhaps, an intimacy in that exchange, which we gloss over through ritual but can never completely erase? Perhaps a wondering if the gift is worthy or we are worthy of receiving it? Or might it be in that moment of giving that I am in touch with you, the giver, and in that moment of receiving know your yearning heart opens to all we can offer you? Amen.

Adapted from *Valparaiso University Prayer Book*, 2001, p. 64

> *For once you were darkness, but now in the Lord you are light. Live as children of light – for the fruit of the light is found in all that is good and right and true.*
>
> *(Ephesians 5: 8-9)*

SHARING THE LIGHT WITHIN THE VU COMMUNITY
Light for campus life
Faith and worship

In remembrance of one's baptism

Heavenly Father,

I thank you for the caring hand and outstretched arm that brought baptismal water to my forehead. Thanks, as well, for those who brought me to the font.

Through this Sacrament, you named and claimed me as your own, invading my space to wash away my sin, and permitting me to start anew at the foot of your cross.

Remind me daily of this gift, that I may never forget the depths of your love for me. By your spirit, enable me to live a life dead to sin and alive in Christ. Through your Son, the same Jesus Christ, who has redeemed me to be a slave to righteousness. Amen.

Confession and forgiveness

Holy God,

You pierce the darkness and know the night of my secrets. Light a candle in my heart to see all that offends you and finds me far from your presence. Show me the light of your grace. In that light, wash me in the basin of your love.

Forgive me, I pray!

Holy Spirit, create in me a restored heart with the capacity to forgive others. Confront me with the blessing of my redemption that I may be a candle's flame revealing your love to the loveless through Jesus Christ, my Lord, who hears my prayer. Amen.

SHARING THE LIGHT WITHIN THE VU COMMUNITY
Light for campus life
Faith and worship

Before receiving the Lord's Supper

Gracious God,

You invite me once again. Before me is the bread of life and the cup of salvation, the very body and blood of Jesus offered for me, a poor sinner.

How can it be that I am called to partake of the bread that is boundless, a guest at the wedding feast of Christ? Lord, I am not worthy to come to your table. Yet, only say the word, and I shall be healed. Prepare my heart to be a lowly manger and a humble cross, that I may receive you as you also receive me.

In this meal, help me to become what I receive, love crucified and love freely given. Until at last, when I shall sit at the Lamb's high feast, glorifying and praising you, O Christ, the Bread of Life. Amen.

After receiving the Lord's Supper

Ever-present Jesus,

Your invitation, gracious and open, has once more nourished me. I am strengthened by your promise to be with all who receive your body and blood. Sustain my energy to live in your presence.

As with your last supper with your disciples, now help me to follow a life of discernment, obedience, and sacrifice. You did not balk when called upon to do your Father's will and take a most difficult path. So inspire and direct me, that I may follow you. Shape my life around daily repentance and daily service of those lost, confused and hurting. Ever-present Jesus, thank you for receiving and sending me in your name. Amen.

SHARING THE LIGHT WITHIN THE VU COMMUNITY
Light for campus life
Faith and worship

For devotional reading of Scripture

Father of all creation,

You have given us the wonderful gift of your Scripture, a book of promises through which we encounter the living Christ. What a treasured resource to have by my side.

Grant that I may be guided today and every day by the power, strength, and hope your Scripture brings to me. I am anxious to learn all that you would teach me. As I study and meditate on your Word, I pray that I might also apply it to my life and be a messenger of your good works. Amen.

Attending Morning Prayer

Almighty Lord,

Thank you for providing me the opportunity to join with this community in prayer. I am grateful there is a time in the day for all of us to gather. Bless the leaders, speakers, and musicians who serve us.

Even when it is difficult, help me to set distractions aside. Please enable me to recognize that which keeps me from feeling at peace. As I spend this time in prayer and worship, may my thoughts be directed toward you and my eyes opened to what you would have me discover. Draw me ever to a closer walk with you. Amen.

For those who preach

Gracious God,

What a daunting task! Whether speaking to a group of 15 or 315, it is no easy matter to proclaim your Gospel.

Be with those who spend arduous hours preparing. Provide them a window into the needs of their listeners.

SHARING THE LIGHT WITHIN THE VU COMMUNITY
Light for campus life
Faith and worship

Guide their words to balance the admonishing word of your law and the affirming word of your Gospel. Keep the cross of Jesus central in their speaking.

Thank you, gracious God, for the proclamations of Moses, Joshua, David, your many prophets, Peter, Paul, Augustine, the long line of church fathers and mothers, Luther, and those in our midst you have raised up with the ability and attitude to stimulate and nurture. May those who speak ever lift up Jesus' life, death, and resurrection. Amen.

For those who do not attend worship

Lord of all,

Pour out grace and mercy upon those who struggle to worship you. Open their hearts and minds to see beyond whatever separates them from you.

When they are tempted to believe only in themselves, lead them to a community of your people. Help them to know what it is to be a part of your worshipping family; let them experience the joy and life that comes from Christian fellowship, receiving the sacraments, and lifting thankful praise to you.

Sometimes, Lord, I am among the errant who do not attend worship. It is so easy to drift away. In such times, spare us all. Speak to us in ways that draw us back to you and one of your worshipping communities.

Stir those who do attend worship to welcome all fully, conveying your non-judging love. Through such expressions of acceptance, may all come to trust you and know you as the One whose arms are always open. Amen.

SHARING THE LIGHT WITHIN THE VU COMMUNITY
Light for campus life
Faith and worship

Christian congregations in Valparaiso

God of love and mercy,

In and around Valparaiso there are worshipping communities of many kinds. Help me to find a congregation where your gracious love is evident.

May they each be receptive to me and to other students who attend their services. Raise up people who will welcome us in the name of Jesus.

Guide me to respond as a fellow member of your holy body. Even if visiting only once, may your Spirit work in all so we may experience the joy of Christian community.

Embolden each of these communities of faith to pursue a mission that binds the wounds of the injured, uplifts the poor, responds to the widowed and imprisoned, and gives hope and courage to outcasts. Remember the leadership of all congregations in this community, that it may be worthy of its calling and models of your way of living. In Jesus' name. Amen.

For my home congregation

Sometimes my home congregation can seem so far away, Lord. Yet, there I learned of your enduring love and mercy. These are the people, however imperfect, who invested in me and nurture my family even today. I feel a kinship, a closeness that comes from shared moments of worship, fellowship, and service.

Still, my home congregation puzzles me at times. Normally so full of generous, forward-looking people, it can become halting, cautious, and full of doubts. In spite of its weaknesses and quirks, I still treasure this congregation of your people.

SHARING THE LIGHT WITHIN THE VU COMMUNITY
Light for campus life
Faith and worship
Prayer is. . .

As years pass and I am less and less involved, grant my church patience in struggle, strength in burdens, endurance in labors, and love in conflict. Continue to bless its members as they take on challenges and make changes. May they be a beacon of light in my home community whom the darkness cannot overcome. Amen.

Prayer is. . .

. . . "When we are praying the liturgal prayers
of the Church, uniting in praise,
we are loving God.
And because we are praying together,
we are loving each other."
– *Mel Piehl from* House of Hospitality *(1938)*

. . . giving ourselves to relationship with God
– a relationship that begins in the heart of God
who longs for communion and communication
with us. Praying – talking and listening
and being in God's presence – reminds us
to attune ourselves more and more to God,
whose love encircles all. – *Louise Williams*

. . . an awareness of God that dispels all fear,
leads us to silence, and awakens us to speech:
to silence of heart, in which we listen
for the direction of God for our lives;
to speech, by which, in all candor, we bring
to the heart of God both our lamentations
and petitions, and our expressions of thanksgiving
and praise. – *Mark W. Bartusch*

Trusting God right now

Dear God,

I'm really struggling to trust you. Following your will for my life can be so unclear at times. Right now it seems like everything is going wrong, and I have trouble seeing your guiding hand in my life. I try and try to master life's challenges on my own, but down deep I know that I can't. Please help me to trust your still, small voice in my life. I desperately need your guidance right now, yet it is unnerving to realize that my life is not in my own hands. Grant me the peace and patience I need to trust you and your love again and again. Amen.

Our many callings

Lord,

We give thanks that each one of us is created to have a purpose in your world. Help us understand our many roles and positions as callings. In you, all are significant.

Please guide us when thinking about our callings, that we may walk the path you lay before us each day. In our lives and labors, stir us to bring your love to all people. Whatever our positions or roles may be, show us how we can serve you. Let your voice, Lord, sing above the pulls of this world and call us to action, whatever it may be, that reveals you to the world. Amen.

For the right choice

Dear God,

What should I do? I have so many choices to make.

How can I best follow you and serve my neighbor? Everyone wants me to do something different but what do you want me to do, Lord?

Show me your way, Lord.

Open my eyes, my ears, and my heart to
your direction.

Help me to wisely weigh my responsibilities, my gifts and
talents, and the choices before me.

Give me the strength to make a decision and the grace
to move forward, trusting in your presence in my life.

Amen.

For guidance regarding my future

God of all time,

You tell us that you have a plan for every individual. Sometimes,
though, I cannot understand what my future holds, and I am
aware of my need for your guidance. It can be so difficult to
see your will for me as I try to sort through the confusion and
consider everything that weighs in my decisions. Please guide
me through your Word, and open me to hear your voice through
others in my life. Lord, help me remember that if I live in you,
you will use me and shape me according to your plan, whatever
the situation. Amen.

For a difficult decision

Father –

My mind is a knot. My breathing is heavy.

My heart aches to know your will for my life.

I need your direction and wisdom as I try to decide which road
I should take.

Oh God, give me insight to ask the right questions and to
understand the impact of my decision upon others.

Remind me that you are with me each step of the journey, and each misstep as well.

Grant me your light in the midst of my darkness so that finally my decision may be made with a courage and confidence that comes from knowing
that I am your child,
that you are my Father,
and that you will always take care of me.

Calm my fears.
Ease my doubts.
And send me your peace. Amen.

First-year student

Father God,

My dream has become reality. I'm a university student!

Why, then, do I have such mixed feelings?

Some days I relish the opportunity to be on my own, or with others my age, whenever and wherever I want. I love the stimulation of good teachers and interesting peers, almost all of whom are new to me.

On other days I feel as if I never left high school. Some classes don't interest or challenge me, and my new circle of friends doesn't always behave like the adults I thought we'd have become by now.

Still, even in disappointing times, I thank you, God, for all the opportunities before me. Lots of people, especially my family, sacrificed plenty to get me here.

Thank you for all who love me. Make me a good friend, especially when my classmates are homesick, burdened with too many questions, or uncertain about why they came to college in the first place.

Use me as an instrument of your love. Amen.

Wrestling with God

We are wrestling, God, and I feel out of joint, like Jacob in the wilderness. I come seeking your blessing.

Here I am God, but where are you?

I was seeking you, and you, I was certain, were leading me.

I am not certain of anything anymore.

Do I even want to believe that you are here?

If you *are* here, it would mean that you are not who I thought you were.

Who are you, God?

If you cannot tell me, stay with me till I know. Let us not stop wrestling until you bless me. Amen.

Choosing a major

Lord of creation,

I know that choosing a major doesn't totally determine my future, but it certainly feels that way!

Help me realize that my major provides me a way to view your world, and a way to learn with a particular community of peers.

Let whatever major I choose help me see the places where your creation shows forth your glory and where it groans for healing.

Whatever I choose, let my major be an avenue to serve you. And let it take me to places that you will, places that I never could have anticipated when choosing it. Amen.

Preparing for a church vocation

Lord God,

Just as when you called your servants Moses and Jeremiah into your service, so now we who follow your call feel inadequate and overwhelmed. We ask that you would free us from our concerns over how fit we may be to serve you as full-time servants, and lead us to trust that your Spirit will work through us. Confirm our calling to public ministry and help us prepare to travel down this well-worn path on which we now walk. In the name of the One who creates, redeems and comforts. Amen.

When uncertain about staying in school

Heavenly Father,

In your infinite graciousness I ask you to bestow upon me a dose of courage that will remove the cataracts of confusion currently clouding my vision and attitude toward my education.

When I question whether I should stay in school, instill in me a sense of immediate and lasting gratitude toward those who have made innumerable sacrifices to ensure my place in life. Grant me clarity to keep their selflessness in the front of my mind with every decision I make.

I want for nothing, Lord. Let me want for nothing more than to succeed for you and all others who've made my schooling and dreams possible. Amen.

> *Do not be conformed to this world, but be transformed by the renewing of your minds, so that you may discern what is the will of God – what is good and acceptable and perfect. (Romans 12:2)*

To ask or not to ask

Guiding Lord,

Most decisions in my life I can handle. You gave me the brain and heart to think clearly and feel empathetically.

What's before me, though, is the biggest decision of my life to date - asking someone to be my life's partner.

Am I ready? Are we ready? Are our families ready?

Then there is the matter of timing. What setting? And how to ask?

But first, thank you for bringing us together, for guiding us through the ups and downs of courtship!

As in so many other decisions, I am looking for positive signs. Calm my mind and heart. If this is the time, excite my creativity and embolden me to ask with confidence, joy and hope. I pray in Jesus' name. Amen.

Graduate school: now or later?

Gracious Lord,

Lots of my classmates are making plans after graduation. Some of them already have job offers. Others have applied to graduate school or a volunteer ministry position.

You know how often I have thought about graduate work. It is not a matter of whether to go, but of when to go.

Time is slipping away. Scholarship deadlines are approaching. I need to make up my mind. Do I apply for graduate school now or later?

Help me sort through all the conflicting advice, all the options, all the pros and cons of now or later. It is time to be decisive, Lord. With you at my side, I am convinced the path will become clear. I pray that it will be so. Amen.

A prayer to open a meeting

Heavenly Father,

We come to you this day amid busy schedules, deadlines, and the pressures and worries of this week. We ask that you fill us with your perfect peace, granting us clarity of mind, renewed energy, and the endurance to carry us through this meeting.

As we gather here to inform, discuss ideas, and make plans, we ask that your presence truly fill this space, guiding us as we work together. Free us from getting bogged down in unuseful agendas that will inhibit our efforts.

In all we do, may our words and actions be a reflection of your abiding love and mercy. Amen.

A prayer to close a meeting

Gracious Lord Jesus,

We thank you for the time we have had together in this meeting – listening, talking, laughing, working, and enjoying each others' ideas and friendships. Please bless all the decisions we have made, that they may accomplish your purpose and further your kingdom. Keep us from actions and attitudes that will undo what we have pursued today.

We thank you for the gifts of those gathered around this table, and we ask now that you be with each of us as we depart. Let no harm befall us in the days ahead. May all praise, honor, and glory be yours now and forever. Amen.

> *And let us consider how to provoke one another to love and good deeds, not neglecting to meet together, as is the habit of some, but encouraging one another, and all the more as you see the Day approaching.*
> *(Hebrews 10:24-25)*

SHARING THE LIGHT WITHIN THE VU COMMUNITY
Light for campus life
The world around us

Live out the gospel

Gracious God,

Open my heart to the majesty of your incomprehensible love.
I praise you for your grace and mercy.

God, empower me to share this love and compassion with others.
Help me be your hands and feet of service. Fashion my words to
be filled with grace. Guide me to share your freeing gospel with
those who are distraught, in despair or who don't know you.

Work in my life so that I may be a blessing to others. In the
compassionate name of Jesus, I pray. Amen.

Prayer for living out vocation

Almighty Triune God,

You have called me by name, blessed me with fruits of the Spirit,
and sent me into the world to be your servant.

Heavenly Father, come. Watch over your servant.

Help me to fill the world's deep hunger through the work that
gives me deep gladness. Guide and protect me from harm as I
enter the broken world to serve you.

Jesus Christ, come. Walk beside your servant.

Stay with me in the trials that I will face in the world. Forgive me
my pride, and humble me to be a more gracious servant.

Holy Spirit, come. Inspire your servant.

Fill me with a deeper desire to share my faith with those I
encounter. Daily renew in me the calling to serve you in all I do.
Amen.

SHARING THE LIGHT WITHIN THE VU COMMUNITY
Light for campus life
The world around us

Addressing the world's ills

Lord almighty,

There is so much hatred, violence, and pain in our world. I cannot stand it or do enough to alleviate it, so I lift up the world's hurts to you, Lord.

Help those who are working to stop war and conflict, who are seeking reconciliation among embittered people, who are putting in hours building up people and communities, and who have enduring optimism that things can change. Encourage them when their optimism is shaken, and open all of our eyes to those moments of hope that highlight your work in the world.

If I can be of help in this work, Lord, my hands, my feet, and my heart are ready and willing. And if you cannot use me tomorrow, or the next day, shape my path so that I am learning and growing in the ways needed to answer the world's ills in the future. Amen.

For justice

Jesus, friend of the outcasts and hope for the despairing,

Grant us the generosity to give fish to all who are hungry. Help us to teach others to fish, so they may be empowered.

Give us the wisdom to stop polluting the pond and the fortitude to tear down the fences that have been built around it, so that all may have access to the goodness of your creation.

Grant us the humility to listen to the stories of outcasts and the despairing, so that we may likewise be fed by their wisdom and insight. In so doing, may we be signs of the coming of your kingdom of peace and justice, and may we love with the same passionate, radical love that you have shown to us. In your life-giving name. Amen.

SHARING THE LIGHT WITHIN THE VU COMMUNITY
Light for campus life
The world around us

same passionate, radical love that you have
shown to us. In your life-giving name. Amen.

Racial harmony

Dear heavenly Father,

We need you now more than ever to teach us to love one another,
to heal us from the deep hatred so many people have because
of racial differences. This world is filled with those who do not
understand the devastating effects of racism, and who simply
seek to be tolerant of others. So many have failed to see people
of other races for who they truly are, your beautiful children,
human beings made in your image. Lord, give us all the strength
to love with an open heart and help us to live in genuine peace
and harmony. In your holy name. Amen.

For nations at war

Lord,

When we see nations caught in the seemingly endless cycle
of war, you bring us hope through your son Jesus Christ, who
was crucified and rose again to break the hold of greed, revenge,
and retribution that grips the world. Help us and our leaders to
recall and understand Christ's message of peace and to be willing
participants and advocates of dialogue rather than warfare. Help
us to remember that our daily actions shape the world in which
we live, and to recall that Christ's commandment was to love those
who hate us.

Guide us with the daily help of the Holy Spirit to build the peace
we long for in our hearts, that nations might be transformed by
Christ working through us, and that love continue to be the light
shining in the darkness. For Jesus' sake. Amen.

SHARING THE LIGHT WITHIN THE VU COMMUNITY
Light for campus life
The world around us

Materialism

Father God,

My life seems to be full of opportunities to buy, to collect, and to possess. With every new day, these opportunities and possessions become more and more alluring and available. At times, I fall into these traps. Forgive me.

As the world around me continues to invest in possessions and wealth, grant me the wisdom to seek value where it truly lies. Help me find contentment in your presence in my life.

Rather than purchasing my status in this world, may I find peace in my status as your child. Sustain me, Lord, in this blessed worth, that I may humbly and gratefully honor your name with all that you have given me. In the name of Jesus Christ your son, my savior, I pray. Amen.

When I have and others do not

Guide me as I seek to follow your example, Jesus.

Remind me of those without a warm bed, those with hunger pains in their stomachs, those with no steady income, those who have been left to fend for themselves, and those who feel abandoned. Let me see them as my brothers and sisters, when I fall asleep in a comfortable dorm room, swipe my meal card in a bountiful cafeteria, learn from advisors and professors, and am surrounded by a community built to support me.

Inspire me to step out of my world of comfort and use my resources to be one with those who have little or none.
Teach me how to bring your love and hope. Amen.

SHARING THE LIGHT WITHIN THE VU COMMUNITY
Light for campus life
The world around us

Devastating disease

Jesus,

Throughout your public ministry you responded to those devastated by disease – the leper, the bleeding, the blind and deaf, the paralyzed, and the haunted.

All came seeking your attention and healing. You gave hope, new perspective and a restored life. You welcomed the outcast into your Father's kingdom, full of promise, peace and purpose.

Today, our world continues to be wracked by devastating disease. There are some new names, like cancer and AIDS, but the impact is the same. Those afflicted face despair, hopelessness, pain and isolation.

Provide courage, dear Jesus, so my friends and I may forge a response, however insignificant and limited. Move us beyond passivity and observation to acts of kindness, generosity and encouragement. Teach us to take up the plight of those devastated by disease in our own varied callings. In your attending and healing name, we pray. Amen.

Respecting and enhancing all of life

Creator and sustainer of all that is,

What a gift you have given to humankind: a universe teeming with life, wonderfully and intricately made, whether found in the earth or in the air. From the beginning you saw all that you created and proclaimed it "good." And so it is.

Yet human hands, mine included, have not respected and enhanced all that lives as we should. Sometimes inattentive, sometimes ill-advised, sometimes knowingly disrespectful, we have injured and even destroyed the young, the aged, and others less able to defend themselves.

SHARING THE LIGHT WITHIN THE VU COMMUNITY
Light for campus life
The world around us

Guide us to be aware and active in respecting and enhancing all of life, Creator God. When difficult decisions confront us, lead us to err on the side of those with little voice and value. Keep us from behavior that enhances only a few at the expense of many. Lead us to calm, yet effective, ways to sustain all that makes this grand world so much of a reflection of you. Amen.

International students

Father in heaven,

Your world teems with people of many nations and places. Like Abraham of old, some of your children have traveled far to realize their hopes.

May those studying in our midst enjoy health, intellectual growth and opportunities for spiritual engagement. Strengthen each international student to persevere in the lonely times and to find a welcoming and hospitable spirit in me and my classmates.

As members of the worldwide community of students, please bless their efforts to achieve their personal and academic goals. Keep their families well and encouraged by what they hear of their academic progress and of our campus.

In the name of Jesus, we commend all international students, whether on our campus or others. Amen.

For the Christian Church

Most holy and merciful Father,

We give you heartfelt thanks for causing people from every ethnic group to become members of God's household, built on the foundation of the apostles and prophets, with Christ Jesus himself as the chief cornerstone. (Ephesians 2:19-20)

SHARING THE LIGHT WITHIN THE VU COMMUNITY
Light for campus life
The world around us

We pray that your Spirit might inspire those who preach the Gospel and illumine those who hear it, that your household may become full to overflowing (Luke 14:23, Romans 11:25), and that together with all your saints we might attain to the whole measure of the fullness of Christ (Ephesians 4:13), and welcome the return of your Son (Matthew 24:14), in whose name we pray. Amen.

For those who serve in the Church

O Lord God,

In this time of ever-increasing cynicism in and about your Church, and the ever-present criticism of those servants who labor in your name, help me to support all ordained, commissioned, and lay workers. Grant to current and future servants the wisdom and perseverance to answer criticism appropriately, the courage to preach your Gospel to even the most critical of people, and the patience to listen and to learn from all who would offer their opinion. In the name of him who has always been patient with us. Amen.

For Christian hope

Almighty and gracious God,

So easily and so often we despair in the presence of our weakness matched against the world's overwhelming terrors. More often than not, we add to the chaos and darkness. We have no hope, except in you. By the power of your Spirit, lift us from the pit of our sins and sorrows, and make of us a living sign that in the reign of your crucified and risen Son, hopelessness cannot rule over us. In Jesus' name we pray. Amen.

Blessings before and after a meal

Traditional Lutheran table prayer

Come, Lord Jesus, be our guest,
and let thy gifts to us be blessed. Amen

Traditional Catholic table prayer

Bless + us, O Lord, and these thy gifts
which we are about to receive from thy bounty
through Christ our Lord. Amen.

Be present

Be present at our table, Lord
Be here and everywhere adored
Thy mercies bless and grant that we
May strengthened for thy service be. Amen.

Blessings after a meal

O give thanks unto the Lord for he is good, for his mercy
endures forever. Amen.

We thank you, O Lord,
for these gifts and for all the gifts
we have received from your goodness,
through Christ our Lord. Amen.

Doxology

Praise God from whom all blessings flow
Praise him all creatures here below
Praise him above ye heavenly host
Praise Father, Son, and Holy Ghost. Amen.

Expressions of Worship

Invocation

We begin in the name of the Father and of the Son + and of the Holy Spirit. Amen.

The Canticle of Zechariah (Benedictus)

Blessed are you, Lord, the God of Israel, you have come to your people and set them free.

You have raised up for us a mighty Savior, born of the house of your servant David.

Through your holy prophets, you promised of old to save us from our enemies, from the hands of all who hate us,

to show mercy to our forebears, and to remember your holy covenant.

This was the oath you swore to our father Abraham, to set us free from the hands of our enemies,

free to worship you without fear, holy and righteous before you, all the days of our life.

And you, child, shall be called the prophet of the Most High, for you will go before the Lord to prepare the way,

to give God's people knowledge of salvation by the forgiveness of their sins.

In the tender compassion of our God the dawn from on high will break upon us,

to shine on those who dwell in darkness and the shadow of death, and to give our feet into the way of peace.   (Luke 1:68-79)

Evangelical Lutheran Worship, Morning Prayer: Gospel Canticle

105

Prayer of confession

Holy and gracious God,

I confess that I have sinned against you this day. Some of my sin I know – the thoughts and words and deeds of which I am ashamed – but some is known only to you. In the name of Jesus Christ I ask forgiveness. Deliver and restore me, that I may rest in peace.

By the mercy of God we are united with Jesus Christ, and in him we are forgiven. We rest now in his peace and rise in the morning to serve him.

Lutheran Book of Worship, Prayer at the Close of the Day: Compline

Prayer before a Crucifix

Behold, O good and most sweet Jesus,

I fall upon my knees before Thee,
and with most fervent desire beg and beseech Thee
that Thou wouldst impress upon my heart a lively sense of
faith, hope and charity,
true repentance for my sins,
and a firm resolve to make amends.
And with deep affection and grief,
I reflect upon Thy five wounds,
having before my eyes that which Thy prophet David spoke about
Thee,
O good Jesus: "They have pierced my hands and feet, they have
counted all my bones." Amen.

Litany of Reconciliation
Cross of Nails, Coventry Cathedral, Center for Reconciliation

All have sinned and fallen short of the glory of God.
The hatred which divides nation from nation, race from race,
class from class,
Father forgive.

The covetous desires of people and nations
to possess what is not their own,
Father forgive.

The greed which exploits the work of human hands and lays waste
the earth,
Father forgive.

Our envy of the welfare and happiness of others,
Father forgive.

Our indifference to the plight of the imprisoned, the homeless,
the refugee,
Father forgive.

The lust which dishonors the bodies of men, women and children,
Father forgive.

The pride that leads us to trust in ourselves and not in God,
Father forgive.

Be kind to one another, tender-hearted, forgiving one another,
as God in Christ forgave you.

Apostles' Creed

I believe in one God, Father Almighty,
     maker of heaven and earth.

And in Jesus Christ, God's only Son, our Lord,
     who was conceived by the Holy Spirit
          born of the virgin Mary
     suffered under Pontius Pilate
          was crucified, died, and was buried.
     He descended into hell.
The third day He rose again from the dead.

He ascended into heaven
> and sits at the right hand of God the Father
> Almighty.
> From thence He will come to judge the living and
> the dead.

I believe in the Holy Spirit,
> the holy catholic church,
> the communion of saints,
> the forgiveness of sins,
> the resurrection of the body, +
> and the life everlasting. Amen.

Valparaiso University Chapel

Before receiving the Lord's Supper

Almighty God, unto whom all hearts be open, and all desires known, and from whom no secrets are hid: cleanse the thoughts of our hearts by the inspiration of thy Holy Spirit: that we may perfectly love thee, and worthily magnify thy holy name: through Christ our Lord. Amen.

Book of Common Prayer, 1549

After receiving the Lord's Supper

We give thanks to you, almighty God, that you have refreshed us with this salutary gift; and we pray that in your mercy you will strengthen our faith in you, and in fervent love toward one another; through Jesus Christ, your dear son, our Lord, who lives and reigns with you and the Holy Spirit, ever one God, world without end. Amen.

Martin Luther (1483-1546)

Holden Evening Prayer

God of mercy, hold us in love.

In peace, in peace, we pray to you:
God of mercy, hold us in love.

For peace and salvation, we pray to you:
God of mercy, hold us in love.

For peace between nations, for peace between peoples:
God of mercy, hold us in love.

For us who are gathered to worship and praise you:
God of mercy, hold us in love.

For all of your servants who live out your gospel:
God of mercy, hold us in love.

For all those who govern, that justice might guide them:
God of mercy, hold us in love.

For all those who labor in service to others:
God of mercy, hold us in love.

Grant weather that nourishes all of creation;
God of mercy, hold us in love.

Keep watch on our loved ones and keep us from danger:
God of mercy, hold us in love.

For all the beloved who rest in your mercy:
God of mercy, hold us in love.

Help us, comfort us, all of our days:
Keep us, hold us, gracious God.

Prayer at the close of the day

Lord, now you let your servant go in peace; your word has been fulfilled. My own eyes have seen the salvation which you have prepared in the sight of every people: a light to reveal you to the nations and the glory of your people Israel. Glory to the Father, and to the Son, and to the Holy Spirit; as it was in the beginning, is now, and will be forever. Amen.

Lutheran Book of Worship, Prayer at the Close of the Day: Compline

Irish blessing

May the road rise up to meet you.
May the wind always be at your back.
May the sun shine warm upon your face,
and rains fall soft upon your fields.
And until we meet again,
May God hold you in the palm of His hand.

Prayer of sending

Lord God,

You have called your servants to ventures of which we cannot see the ending, by paths as yet untrodden, through perils unknown. Give us faith to go out with good courage, not knowing where we go, but only that your hand is leading us and your love supporting us; through Jesus Christ our Lord. Amen.

Lutheran Book of Worship, Evening Prayer: Vespers

Benediction

May the Lord bless us and keep us,
May the Lord make his face shine upon us and be gracious to us,
May the Lord look upon us with favor and grant us peace.
Amen.

Move in day

Lord,

Thank you for those helping move me in and for the new opportunity college brings. Though this is an experience sure to bring positive changes, today is frightening.

As I leave my family to forge new relationships, comfort and embolden me. As I make this room my home for this year, help me to be a fair and faithful roommate. Bless our relationship.

Please be with me as I meet my floormates. Bless these relationships, too. Mold us to recognize when another needs a shoulder to lean on or someone to listen. Guide us all through this new experience. Amen.

Opening Convocation Hymn

O God, our help in ages past
Our hope for years to come,
Our shelter from the stormy blast,
And our eternal home:

Under the shadow of your throne,
Your saints have dwelt secure:
Sufficient is your arm alone,
And our defense is sure.

Before the hills in order stood,
Or earth received its frame,
From everlasting you are God,
To endless years the same.

O God, our help in ages past,
Our hope for years to come,
Still be our guard while troubles last
And our eternal home!

Lutheran Book of Worship #320 v 1-3, 6; text by Isaac Watts, 1674-1748; alt.

Beginning a sports season

Dear Lord,

We give thanks for the blessings that you have bestowed upon the athletic teams of Valparaiso University. Let us be a light to others wherever we compete. May we represent the University and you, Lord God, in all we do.

As the season unfolds, keep us from harm as we compete, and bring quick healing to those who suffer injury. Weld those who form the team, that we may encourage and challenge one another to excel. Spare us envy, strife, and irritation in all we do on and off the field of play. Let all our efforts be to glorify your name. Amen

Celebrating Founders Day

God of all ages,

Even though our tendency to self-centeredness draws us to the matters of today, turn our hearts and minds to yesteryear and to others' contributions and courage that linger even now. We seek to remember those you moved to shape and launch Valparaiso University. We wish to learn from their struggles and defeats while relishing their bold efforts and grand successes.

Fill our recollections, and celebration, with gratitude, hope, and resolve.

Kindle in us gratefulness for those who led, administered, and taught in years past.

Spur in us hope that looks back and gains energy, perspective, and determination.

Stir in us resolve to make our best contribution, however daunting the challenge.

May we together further the educational mission that unites us. In the name of the One who came to serve. Amen.

St. Teresa's Café Manna

Lord, we give you thanks
    For the gifts you have bestowed upon us,
For shelter and food,
    For clothing and comfort.
We ask that you watch over those people
    Whose lives are touched by Café Manna.
For those who come in need of a warm meal
    And warm smiles,
For those who offer their time to help cook
    And to serve those less fortunate.
Lord, we ask that all who gather at this place
    Might know that you are there alongside
        Each and every one of us.
Bless us, O Lord, and grant that all who gather
    May one day feast at your heavenly banquet. Amen.

Intramurals

Dear God,

Bless this time of competition that I am enjoying with my friends.
Let me play my hardest while holding sportsmanship paramount.

As I engage in this amiable pastime, I ask you to watch over all
on the field of play, that we may be free from injury. Keep us from
misunderstanding and overly aggressive actions.

Father, help me and my friends keep this game in perspective.
When the final whistle blows, turn our heads to congratulations
and playful conversation. May we see these intramurals as another
way to exercise, enjoy friendships, and use our physical abilities.
Amen.

Homecoming

Heavenly Father,

Thank you for this day and for this place I am beginning to call home more and more often. Thank you for the founders' vision of a university that combines faith and learning. Watch over those in this community – fellow students, faculty, administrators, and alumni – and in the home I am leaving behind – family and friends. As I celebrate homecoming, please forgive any excesses of the weekend and remind me of the blessings in store at your grand, final homecoming. For then, surely, in your light, we see light. Amen.

Shack City

God, our provider and protector,

We find ourselves tonight in fragile boxes that resemble what some people call homes. Strengthen the community we build here this evening so that Valparaiso might be moved to use some of its resources to offer supportive communities and sturdier buildings for homes.

Open our hearts to the strangers we meet and guide the speakers, singers, and all the participants to share the warm hospitality of your love during the cold night. Amen.

Family weekend

Father,

Thank you for the blessings that you have bestowed upon me through the love and support of my family. I am so grateful for each person in my family. They have been a rock for me as Peter was for your church.

May this weekend be a special time for all families gathered on campus. Help us enjoy being together, and provide everyone a safe return home. Lord, please kindle our love for each other and for

you, that our lives may reflect your goodness and mercy. Amen.

Advent Christmas Vespers

God, whom we await and in whom we live,

As your servants gather for Advent Christmas Vespers, let us all prepare our hearts and minds for the celebration of your incarnation. Watch over your servants, especially sacristans, acolytes, choirs, and ministers, who prepare the church for contemplation and praise. Bring your people together from far and wide, Lord, so we may await your coming, the advent of Jesus. Praise to you, O Lord, and may your Church be ever watchful. Amen.

Christmas concert

Dear Lord,

Tonight we gather to celebrate the birth of your son, our Saviour, Jesus Christ. We pray that our gift of music will shine with the holy presence of your name and the joyfulness we feel as we celebrate Jesus' birth. With your divine blessing we pray that our hearts may be ever open to sing and play with the hope that comes only through our relationship to you. Hold us this night in your loving care and be with all who hear melody and word, that they may be refreshed anew with the promise of God with us. In the name of the holy Christ Child, we pray. Amen.

Finals

Understanding and attentive God,

Another time of testing is approaching. You have been with me so far; please remain with me through the finals that are before me.

Now I must taste the fruits of my semester's labor. Some weeks I have been focused and on top of my assignments. Other weeks my efforts have been sluggish and second-best.

Still, I seek to finish strong. I promise to give my best. All I ask is that you would keep me alert and bless my efforts. Amen.

Starting another semester

Here we go again, God. Dare I mention that the break was too short? Nevertheless, it is good to be back. This is my vocation, God. It's where I belong at this point in my life. It's where you have put me. Help me not forget that, as I grit my teeth and wade into campus life and academic responsibilities once more. Keep my eyes open to what you are accomplishing in me during these years. Shape me for ventures ahead, and open those doors that lead into your future. Amen.

Valparaiso University Prayer Book, 2001, p. 92

Martin Luther King, Jr. Day

As we remember the faithful commitment of Dr. Martin Luther King, Jr., give us also we pray, O Lord,

Attentiveness to pain and oppression that others in your world are experiencing;

Perspective for discerning your concerns for troubled and neglected people;

Courage to stand supportively with those in need;

Tenderness in the care of children;

Strength to resist the temptation to turn away; and

Joy to know you are at our side in our striving to be faithful. Amen.

Valparaiso University Prayer Book, 2001, p. 80

Rush

Oh God,

Thank you for this blessed time wherein I am meeting new friends and growing in collegiate fellowship. Rare is it that I get to experience such excitement for free.

Unfortunately, rush is transitory, and at the end of these days I must make a difficult decision. Father, I have made so many good friends in this process, which is making it difficult to figure out which group I should pledge.

Keep me from a decision that is based on externals and illusions. As I seek counsel from others, temper their advice with openness and objectivity. Please guide me to make a choice that is healthy for me and for those whom I will join. In this and all my choices, may your will be done. Amen.

World Relief Campaign

Dear generous and sustaining God,

We thank you for all the blessings we have received and the opportunity we now have through the World Relief Campaign to extend those blessings to more of your children. Excite our hearts for this project, that we may be diligent stewards of the resources we have been given.

Help us to share with those of our community the stories of our brothers and sisters who will be benefited by this campaign, that we may be with them in their struggles. May this project bring them an enduring hope, and may it empower and enliven their community for years to come. In your holy name. Amen.

Relay for Life

Dear God,

Help us to go about our work gracefully, knowing that we aren't able to eradicate suffering and disease from this world. Inspire us to take care of each other, acknowledging pain and providing comfort and support from within this united community. Give us the courage to confront fears and to embrace tears. Guide us to show others through our words and our actions that God's love is powerful enough to have the final say in our lives. Amen.

Spring weekend

It's one of the last big flings of the year, Lord. Loads of planning have gone into spring weekend – concerts, dances, songfest and lots of other doings. Bless all who bear responsibility for things happening well.

Once the weekend is over, I'll really get serious and hit the books. This is a promise.

But for now, Lord, let this weekend be an upbeat, fun and safe time with friends and on-campus guests. Equip us more fully to be for each other what you would have us be. And refresh us for studies ahead. I have a promise to keep. Amen.

Adapted from *Valparaiso University Prayer Book,* 2001, p. 15

Rebuilding Together

Lord,

Thank you so much for this chance to serve our fellow men through Rebuilding Together. Allow us to be your hands and feet as we tackle all the challenges of the day. Keep us smiling, Lord, as we aid those who have no other means of receiving this help. May our efforts permit those who receive our labors realize that you are the source of all goodness, that we, being strangers, are able to love one another through acts of kindness. We pray in your name, the One whose sacrifice inspires us to work on behalf of others. Amen.

Celebrating Easter at the Chapel of the Resurrection

Gracious and merciful God,

We have followed your son Jesus, and all the generations of followers who have gone this way before us, through another week that began with hosannas and rejoicing but then led to places of betrayal, trial, judgment, and death.

Words cannot convey the depth of what we learn about ourselves and about your great mercy each time we make this journey. We give you humble thanks for those who go with us and who in this place and time embody for us the presence of your son.

Last evening in the quiet candlelight of the Vigil, we heard again the sweet and thrilling news of his resurrection. Today, amidst the beautiful music and festive balloons of celebration, we trust in you to gladden our hearts, lift our spirits, and make us new again to live the life of your risen son, Jesus Christ our Lord, who lives and reigns with you and the Holy Spirit, one God, now and always. Amen.

Baccalaureate

Valparaiso, Alma Mater,
Gratefully we sing your praise.

Flame of faith and lamp of learning
Here have form'd our finest days.
Thankful for your founders' vision,
Others too in years to come
Still will find on one fair campus
Athens and Jerusalem.

Father, you have in your image
Form'd us handsomely endow'd.
Send us out to probe your planets,

119

Heal our neighbors, sway the crowd.
Gospel freed from fear of knowledge,
Let us spend our wit and might
Learning, serving, feeding, feasting,
For in your light we see light.
  "Valparaiso, Alma Mater," *Valparaiso University Prayer Book,* 2001, p. 3

Graduation day

Yikes! Help! Thank you! Here we go! Amen.

Saying goodbyes

God,

Thank you for this community – Lord, I am going to miss the people here.

I can hardly believe how far you have brought me, and now we ar taking this next step into only you know what. You are so much more steady than my life is these days.

Keep me steadfastly seeking you when I leave this place. Grant me inspiration, motivation, and humility as I put to use the gifts you have given me. Amen.

Overseas summer study course

God of all nations,

You have brought us to a country that is not our own so that we might learn from its peoples. Help us to respect this part of your creation and to love your children in this place.

Have our hosts teach us how you have been at work in their mids Give us energy to explore the uniqueness of this land and the insight to ask thoughtful questions.

Upon returning home, help us remember what we have discovered, the friendships we have made, and to speak well of those we have met on our travels. Amen.

**Those campus happenings
for which I want to pray...**

_____

_____

_____

_____

_____

_____

_____

_____

_____

_____

_____

_____

_____

_____

_____

Promise

THE PRAYER OF THE RIGHTEOUS
IS POWERFUL AND EFFECTIVE.

JAMES 5:16

Purpose – Praying for others is an honor and privilege. This form of prayer allows one to "intercede" and pray for the needs of others and of the whole world.

Practice – Normally practiced within a worship service, intercessory prayer is a comprehensive way to pray in a personal way. It is one of the oldest practices of prayer.

Process

1. Make a list of happenings and/or individuals (see pages 121 and 214-215) for which you want to pray.

2. Organize your prayer to God with this suggested outline of intercessions: family and friends, the world, the church, your community, the sick and dying, and remembrance of those who died in faith.

3. Set aside time to pray. Begin by thanking and praising God. Then make your intercessions before God.

4. Be attentive to the manner in which God gives answer to your prayers at that time and in the days that follow.

Prayer – Pray that the Holy Spirit help you be aware of the needs of family, friends, the world, the church and your community, the sick and the dying. Remember to pray for a grateful heart.

123

Taking our cares to the Light

The discipline of reflecting on Scripture, taking time to meditate on God's grace, and praying on behalf of ourselves and others are all a part of a vibrant devotional life. A regular prayer life is also a real blessing for a Christian.

Sometimes, however, life confronts us with circumstances that are, for us or for people we are close to, full of crisis.

The following 17 pages are provided for times when the darkness of human folly, fickleness, and faithlessness threaten to overwhelm the light in our lives. Each section addresses an issue that students at Valpo have identified as a struggle of theirs or their friends. These challenges can arise at any point in a student's experience and can afflict male and female alike.

Issues like these can often make us feel isolated. If so, remember this: others have experienced difficulties similar to ours and have, by the grace of God, made their way through them. This itself is good news!

For every issue, there are some introductory thoughts, suggested readings from Scripture, and words of prayer. You can also benefit from the counsel and consolation of your pastors here on campus or back home, as well as from trusted Christian friends, teachers, and mentors.

Beyond even these human resources, it is good to remember the promise given to us through the words of St. Paul:

> *Likewise the Spirit helps us in our weakness; for we do not know how to pray as we ought, but that very Spirit intercedes with sighs too deep for words.* (Romans 8:26)

May it be so today for us.

Loneliness

On one hand, it is kind of weird to be lonely on a residential campus of nearly 3,500 students. On the other hand, when we are surrounded by people who seem to have lots of great company and we do not, the presence of other people can make our sense of isolation that much more unbearable.

It can be a struggle to find our place and our crowd. We can begin to feel unappreciated, even odd, until we remember that we have already got a place and a people.

Take the time to read and think through one or more of the following portions of Scripture:

Hebrews 4:14-16	John 14:1-6
Romans 12:1-8	1 Kings 19:9-18

Perhaps our sense of loneliness is a call to act on faith, faith that the community of Jesus really exists, even for us, in the form of real people who might themselves be struggling with loneliness. Consider taking a bold step by engaging someone who might appreciate interacting with another Christian.

Lord God,

When Elijah was desperate and lonely, you called him from his hiding place with a still, small voice and led him to companionship and your service. Give me ears to hear your call of encouragement to me. Grant me courage to seek out companions among my peers, and a desire to help enrich their lives. In your service. Amen.

Broken relationships

When a relationship, especially a dating relationship, has been broken and you are the one who has been rejected, it is difficult not to take it personally. We like what we had and, most times, we'd like to have it back.

Our desire to hold on to relationships we have had can be compounded by our perception that, as Christians, we are compelled by the Gospel to work for the restoration of relationships that have been broken. We can find ourselves saying and doing some pretty goofy and humiliating things in an effort to get back what we have lost.

In times like these, when our sense of self-worth has taken a real hit, we need to find solid ground. Consider how our creator views us in passages like:

Luke 12:13-21	Colossians 1:9-12
1 Corinthians 7:23	Colossians 3:12-14

Jesus, my comforter and friend,

My heart is breaking over my loss. Be present to me in the community of your Church and in the friends you have given me. Heal my wounds and make me strong again so that my actions in relationships are grounded in your love for me and not in my need to be someone I am not, just to have someone else's approval and affection. In the name of Jesus. Amen.

Overwork and overtraining

In many respects, college is a terrible time to learn good work habits. This is especially true on a residential campus, where there is never really a time when you are not "at work."

Add to this that almost everyone is trying to make the most of their experience; let's face it, VU is, in many ways, a very competitive environment, and the odds of being among overachievers are pretty high.

The pattern of work and rest established by God in the first two chapters of Genesis is worthy of our attention. If the Almighty Maker of heaven and earth finds it worthwhile to rest on the seventh day, is finding a balance between work, play, and rest not something to be sought? After all, each is God's gift to us based on God's goodness, *not* on how hard we work or strive to achieve.

How might these readings inspire us to slow down and take some time to enjoy the life and world God provides?

>   Isaiah 40:28-31
>   Matthew 11:28-30
>   Luke 12:27-30

Almighty One, maker of heaven and earth,

You called your creation "very good" and rested on the seventh day. Inspire me with your grace and show me how to set time apart from my work. Remind me that I am a co-creator with you and not a maker of my own destiny, for you have assured me of my future in the life, death, and resurrection of Jesus. Amen.

Depression

What do we do when the world is closing in around us?
When nothing seems worth the effort and the only thing that
makes any sense is staying in bed? When darkness pervades?

Experiences like these are not what God intends for our lives. In
our clearer moments, it is not what we would wish for ourselves.
Yet, when depressed, there is not much energy or desire to be any
other way.

The writer of Psalm 6 seems to have been in the same spot,
looking at his sorry state and describing it in sad detail. He
pleads with God to hear his cry and come to his rescue. Clearly,
this guy knows the blues intimately. But he also knows deep
down, in a place deeper than his depression, that God will
be his rescue and help.

Maybe you have lost sight of this critical fact in your life, that
God can rescue you from the pits. It is true. Consider, also, Isaiah
43:1-2 and Matthew 6:34 and the story of Jonah, especially his
prayer in Jonah 2.

Take the risk. Tell someone like an RA, a residential minister,
a pastor or a counselor how bad it is and see how God will provide
you with the means of finding your own way into the light.

Lord God,

Hear my cry. Hear my prayer for release, light, and freedom. You
heard the prayer of Jonah and brought him deliverance. Show me
those who stand ready to be your hands of deliverance for me and
give me the courage to tell them of my gloom. Send your Spirit
to help them free me from this darkness. I ask this for the sake
of Jesus, my life and my light. Amen.

Sexual assault

The horror can be so overwhelming. We would like to believe that it did not happen. Worse yet, we tell ourselves that it was, in some way, our fault. We should have said "no" more forcefully, or not have been where we were.

Among the tragedies of sexual assault is the fact that often the victim is seen as responsible for what happened. But the injustice and shame of this situation need not be our undoing. We need not feel stained by our experience.

Paul writes to the Ephesians that Christ offers himself as a sacrifice in order to cleanse them and us (5:25-27). There is no disgrace, no stain, no shame that has not been washed away by the blood of Jesus.

After being assaulted, living God's truth will take some work and some help. A place to start is with the campus SAAFE office. The people who work there care about what has happened and are trained to help. The office crisis line is 219-464-6789 and website is www.valpo.edu/saafe.

There is more. God not only cleanses us from our own sin, but God also cleanses us from the effect of sins that have been committed against us. The following Scripture confirms how God sees us:

John 1:5-7 1 Corinthians 3:16-17

Hear my cry for restoration, O God!

Put away from my mind the terrors of the assault that I have suffered. Remind me that I am your own precious child. By your Spirit's power, instill in me an awareness of my baptism whose cleansing water brings forgiveness and life. Give me strength to seek help soon. When it is time, move me to forgive. Humble, teach, and change my attacker. Guide now my anxious steps and keep me close to you and others who understand. Amen.

Being judgmental

The Bible teaches us to be observant and careful, to evaluate the actions of others in light of God's will for human life. We are called to exercise good judgment regarding the people with whom we associate and spend time.

However, when our assessment of others becomes a near constant in our lives, when we are rarely happy with what others have done, or when we see our dissatisfaction as someone else's problem, then we have probably slipped from exercising sound judgment to being judgmental.

Jesus cautioned his critics who seemed to have no trouble pointing out the sins of others. Rather than point to the speck in someone else's eye, he asked them first to remove the log from their own eye.

Finally, though, it is only the blood of Christ that will overcome even the most notorious of failures and the most judgmental of actions. Jesus' forgiveness can build in us a blessed humility and a foundation for good judgment. Consider the following verses:

> Luke 6:39-42   Luke 15
>
> John 8:1-11   1 Timothy 1:15

O Merciful Lord,

Forgive my tendency to judge others harshly. Remind me that you seek to save the lost rather than condemn all to life without you. Bless me with the assurance of your forgiveness and fill me with a spirit of kindness and grace so that I might act as a bearer of your love and not be an agent of condemnation. I ask this for Jesus' sake. Amen.

In the midst of conflict

Conflict in life is to be expected. In fact it is a result of the freedom that God gave our first parents (Genesis 2). They were free to choose of the trees of the garden. Unfortunately, they valued their desires over following God's command.

Individuals making free choices and having differing values are bound to differ. Sometimes the conflict from selecting a differing choice produces positive results. Other times it produces unhealthy tension and alienation, especially if that decision is hurtful to us.

Our first instinct is to get him or her back, even if it takes us out of our normal character. But violence gives way to violence, and sin in return usually gives birth to more sinful action. It is often not the conflicts themselves that are the problem; it is the hostility and resentment that result.

The following verses, read in order, provide a plan for God-pleasing action in the presence of conflict:

> 1 Corinthians 10:31-33   Matthew 7:3-5
>
> Matthew 18:15-17   Matthew 5:23-24

Can you approach conflicted situations in this way? If you do, may God bless and prosper your efforts.

Lord Jesus,

You have called us to imitate you. Teach me how to be so. In the heat of tense times when disagreement threatens to turn me and others into Satan's servant, let me find a way to be a blessing rather than a curse. Guide my thoughts and words by the Scriptures I have just read, so that all I say and do will contribute to a genuine resolution of conflict and bring peace and glory to your holy name. Amen.

Trouble at home

Trouble at home has a way of invading our dorm room. It can occupy our head and heart. The distance and incomplete communication, even with all our technological gadgets and resources, can combine to make difficulties at home even more stressful for us.

It is tempting to believe that we should rush home and try to fix things. It can also be tempting to believe that our life will come apart if things continue to unravel at home.

As a missionary pastor, St. Paul often left unsettled and unsettling situations with a heavy heart. Even though he could not be present, he trusted that the Spirit of God would be (Philippians 4:4-9). He also knew that his own security lay not in others' reception of his teachings or in their new behavior.

Paul's security, as well as ours, lays in the righteousness of Christ that has been given to us as a gift. This knowledge frees us to focus on the tasks that are at hand.

Consider the following as you try to let go of things you cannot control at home and focus on the work that actually is yours today:

Psalm 23   John 14

Bless my family, O God.

Where there is anger, bring understanding. Where there is division, bring unity. Where there is betrayal, bring forgiveness and trust. Grant my family the strength and determination to survive this difficult time, and help me to do what is useful for my family with patience, wisdom, and courage. In Jesus' name. Amen.

Alcohol and drug use

We have all heard or read about the dangers
of abusing alcohol, tobacco and other "recreational drugs." In spite
of efforts to curb their appeal, these materials continue to have a
powerful presence among us.

It might strike us as odd to regard these substances as among the
gifts of God's creation. But if we are serious when we pray "the
earth is the Lord's and everything in it," it is a hard conclusion
to avoid. The sad fact is this: humanity has a rather uneven record
when it comes to dealing well with God's gifts. This is especially
true regarding patient medications, alcohol, and tobacco, which
can produce significant effects on the brain.

In a culture that seeks quick fixes, and often at an age when we
feel virtually indestructible, it is easy to ignore the dangers that
accompany these substances. Before we know it, they literally
take over our lives and bring us to a place where we love them
more than our own lives, more, even, than God.

If you have been out of control or are afraid that drugs or alcohol
are starting to run your life, that of a friend or family member,
now is the time to seek the help of a trusted friend, a counselor
or pastor. There are people around you who want to help, not
just write you up for a violation of policy.

Proverbs 20:1   Psalm 104

Lord Jesus,

Your creation, which was intended for my blessing, is becoming
a curse for me. I am no longer in control of myself, alcohol/drugs
are. I have forfeited my capacity to be a steward of my life and
be responsible for all of your gifts. Forgive me, Lord. Guide me
to understand my behavior; then give me courage to seek help,
and the determination to live more healthily. Amen.

Sexuality and sexual orientation

It might be hard to believe, given the culture in which we live, but there is more to each of us than our sexuality and/or our sexual orientation. We are a body, mind and soul with God-given gifts to develop and share as we live out our call to praise God and serve humanity.

"You have been bought with a price;" is the way St. Paul puts it. This ownership by God, at the price of Christ's life, is the foundation of our identities, not whom we might date or might fall in love with. As critical as human relationships are for us, and even our romantic wants, they are never the absolute foundation for our being.

While the internal struggle with one's sexuality can be profoundly complicated, and even isolating, there are those, both on and off campus, with whom talking things out can be helpful. Consider, also, the following readings:

Romans 6:1-14   Galatians 3:23-28   Galatians 5:22-23

Lord God my maker,

You have created me for relationships. You know I do not want to be lonely in this world of couples and families. Spare me misdirected activity and unfulfilling relationships. Help me direct my desires and yearnings in ways that bless other persons of your making.

Grant me grace to recognize your presence for me in your Church. Remind me that you are the foundation of my life. Thank you for making me aware and appreciative of friendships and relationships that are wholesome for me. Guard and nurture us all. In the name of Jesus, my brother. Amen.

Lust and pornography

Human beings are created to be in relationships. Some point out that the reality of the Trinity (the idea that God has been revealed to us as three persons that are one god) shows that our need for intimacy is part of God's image in us. Clearly, there is a lot riding on our relationships.

Our need for intimacy is a powerful drive in us. It is so powerful that it can lead us to think things and do things of which we are soon ashamed. When it comes to satisfying our craving for intimacy, we seem to have little trouble transforming those around us, and those in pictures or videos, into objects that we can use for our satisfaction.

So often, when intimacy is really shaky ground for us, we are all the more at risk for objectifying others. We choose this path rather than pursue relationships that call for openness, honesty, and mutuality, which can place us at risk for rejection.

How do the following readings remind us that those whom we have turned into objects to be consumed are, themselves, really beloved sisters and brothers, all cherished by God?

Joel 2:28-29   Luke 10:25-37

Almighty God,

I have made objects out of your children. For the sake of Jesus, forgive me. Recall me to your care and keeping. Turn me from my own raging hunger for and deep fear of intimacy. Heal and free those I have wronged, and challenge me to see them as you do. In the name of Jesus. Amen.

The loss of a loved one

Grieving a loss due to the death of a loved one is hard work. It is often made harder by the false perception that, as Christians, we should be able to get over the loss quickly. After all, Jesus defeated death, right?

Notice that St. Paul does not say a Christian should not grieve. He calls us to grieve as ones who have hope (1 Thessalonians 4:13-18). Death is the awful reminder that the world suffers under the curse of sin.

The death of one we love, awful as it is, is a compelling reminder of our own mortality. Our day will also come when there will be no more breath in us.

For now, we can let our grief take possession of us. But we can grieve without fear, because we know that, in time, our grieving will come to an end. First, as we grow to live with the loss and, then, as we hold on to the promise of the resurrection of all of God's people.

As you go, consider the wisdom and promise of:

Psalm 46   Jonah 2   Romans 6:5

Bless the memory of dear … who is now lost to me. I am grateful for the time that was ours. Comfort all who lament and weep. Help me in the midst of things I cannot understand, to believe and trust in the communion of saints, the forgiveness of sins, and the resurrection to life everlasting. Amen.

A healthy attitude toward weight

It is a well-known fact that pictures of models are routinely adjusted by graphic artists to make the models appear "more beautiful," albeit unreal. Apparently, even those who get paid big money for their good looks, and the people who pay them, are not completely satisfied with the way they look.

Maybe you have not been happy with your weight for a while. It is easy for us to get sucked into believing that changes to our weight will solve all of our problems – especially when we have been dissatisfied for a long time.

There is certainly something to be said for taking care of ourselves, eating well, and being in good shape. But like many good things, concern about weight can become "too much of a good thing" and take on a life of its own. In the end, we can be even more miserable.

The remembrance that Christ loves us just as we are can help to get our concern for our weight back into perspective. For additional perspective, take a look at:

Psalm 139

Help me, O God, my creator and redeemer, to see myself as you see me, now that Jesus has paid the ransom for my life. When I grow dissatisfied with my body, help me to find a gracious vision of myself that celebrates your gifts to me. Lead me to maintain a balance between disciplined self-care and a calm acceptance of who I am. Help me to love myself as I love my neighbor and you, for the sake of Jesus. Amen.

When a friend is mourning

What a helpless feeling! We care about those who are grieving, we can see their pain and we would like nothing more than to help them deal with it.

But nothing we do, it seems, will fix the situation. In fact, the best gift we can give someone who is mourning is not the right remedy to fix things, but a willingness to be with them as they mourn. Having a friend who honors our grief is a gift to be highly valued.

Often for the one who is grieving, the awareness of the deceased is heightened in the days and weeks after the death. The person feels compelled to tell others what made the deceased so special. A friend who listens patiently to these stories, even if they are repeated, gives a real gift. After all, even Jesus listened with compassion to the two heartbroken disciples as they all walked to Emmaus that first Easter evening:

Luke 24:13-35

O Holy Spirit,

Help me to be attentive to my friends as they mourn. Give them courage and strength to work through their loss in the days ahead. Comfort them in ways that meet their needs. Give me a generous heart and a listening ear in the days and weeks ahead, that I may be an example of your deep care. In Jesus' name. Amen.

Procrastination

There are numerous reasons why we procrastinate. One of the most insidious is that whatever we do must be done perfectly. Stymied by less than perfect efforts, we either give up, run out of time, or throw something together at the last moment with the comment, "If I had more time I would have something better, but what's done is done."

Wouldn't it be more helpful to acknowledge that our perfectionism is our doomed attempt to gain acceptance and be seen as special? Is it not another way we attempt to make ourselves worthwhile?

We engage in such fruitless efforts even though we know our worth has been established by God when we were ransomed at the price of Jesus' death. Just remember, while our projects deserve our best efforts, none will ever be *that* good, even if we do start earlier and have lots of time to finish.

Philippians 4:6-9   Philippians 4:13

O God,

Help me with my priorities. Remove from my heart the fear of failure that prevents me from addressing my responsibilities. Guide me as I order my work so that I can make the most of your gifts to me. Give me a healthy perspective on what is realistic while still striving to use my full potential. When my work load becomes overwhelming, provide me the presence of mind to manage my tendency to procrastinate with prayers such as this and a resolve to do my best with the time before me. In the name of Jesus. Amen.

When tempted to lie

It is said that an honest person can get by with a lousy memory. There are not any half-truths or factious stories to keep straight.

We rarely lie for the sheer fun of duping someone. So why do we lie? It is usually because we are trying to protect ourselves or someone else from what would happen if the truth were exposed. In that process, we fear that others will know the real truth about the situation or person and, as a result, will think less of us or of them.

Besides living with the fear of being found out and the need to keep track of false stories, lying has a corroding effect. It destroys our sense of right and wrong, and we rarely stop at one mistruth.

So, when we are tempted to lie to cover something, ask, "Of what or whom are we afraid in this situation?" How can the assurance of the forgiving presence of Christ in our lives help us to respond to these fears?

Proverbs 12:13-21   2 Samuel 12:1-14

Jesus,

You know my heart so much better than I do. Convict me of the foolishness of my fear. Bless my truth-telling. Give me words of sensitivity and integrity. Help me to maintain an openness that is grounded in the security that only your righteousness can provide through the blood of Jesus. Amen.

Nagging guilt

There is an ancient saying, "Christians aren't perfect, just forgiven." This adage can make it feel even worse when feelings of forgiveness remain elusive.

Persistent guilt or the feeling that forgiveness is for others, but not for you, can be really debilitating. Whether you are harboring the knowledge of some secret sin or struggling with the feeling that nothing you do is good enough, there are people around you who are ready to help.

Psychological counselors can help you figure out if your overwhelming sense of guilt is a product of your own unrealistic expectations of yourself or your life. A pastor who hears private confession will give you a place to speak about the real failures that you find so threatening and then help you see that God's forgiveness in Jesus covers even the most conscience-burdening sins.

While you prepare yourself for such conversations, read and pray through the following readings:

1 John 1:8-9   Luke 5:17-26

John 18:15-18, 25-27, 21:15-17

Lord Jesus,

You lived a life of perfect obedience to God's will and suffered death to provide for my forgiveness. Prepare my heart to make confession of that which burdens me so that I might know your grace and mercy. Then, help me live in the peace and freedom that passes all human understanding. Amen.

GOD'S PROMISE TO US IN JESUS CHRIST AFFIRMS
"I am with you always to the end of the age."

promise

| MATTHEW 28:20B |

Lectio Divina – Divine reading

Purpose – *Lectio Divina* is a slow contemplative praying of the Scriptures enabling them to become a means of listening to God.

Practice – *Lectio Divina* is an ancient monastic prayer tradition that has proven through centuries to be inspirational and fulfilling. Instituted by St. Benedict in his "Rule," he teaches how to listen "with the ear of our hearts."

Process – These steps will assist in praying this ancient form personally or as a group:

1. Choose a text from the Bible and then quiet yourself so that you are prepared to hear God's word.

2. Read slowly out loud, listening reverently for the still, small voice of God. Read attentively that you might hear a word or phrase that is God's word for you this day.

3. Once you have discovered a word or phrase that speaks to you in a personal way, "ruminate," which means ponder it by repeating it to yourself and letting it interact with your thoughts, hopes and desires.

4. Now enter into conversation with God, offering yourself to God.

5. Finally, rest in the presence of God. Let the word of God you prayed embrace you as you contemplate in silence. Let go of your own words and enjoy the presence of God!

Prayer – Give thanks to God for the time just given to ponder on this word, and ask for God's abiding presence.

Following the Light through the Days
and Seasons of the Church Year

We of the Valparaiso University community always live in more
than one scheme of time. The one that we're most conscious
of is the rhythms of the academic year. Semesters begin in August
and January; we then fall into a routine of classes and other
activities at certain times on certain days; we take breaks shorter
and then longer (or in the spring longer and then shorter); we
frenetically study, write, and test at the end of the term; and then
we move on for a time to other places and tasks. For good reason,
the greater part of this prayer book focuses on the events and
concerns of the academic year.

But as a Christian academic community we are always
simultaneously part of an older and more widely-lived time
scheme, the church year. While the details of this cycle vary
among Christian traditions, its broad outlines are fixed and
purposeful. The church year retells the story of the decisive
events by which God intervened in the history of the world, fully
human in Jesus Christ. It is a pattern and a discipline, but it is
above all a resource for worship, meditation, and devotion.

The church year also seeks to enable Christians to participate
fully and consciously in the biblical conceptions of time and space
that God's people are "really present" at the events by which God
made them his own, that they might be a blessing to the world.
Thus, Moses instructed Israel to tell their children that God had
spared "our" houses on Passover night in Exodus 12. Later, in
Deuteronomy 5 he spoke to the generation that had been born
in the wilderness as if they had been present at Sinai. Thus, Jesus
prays for the future generations who will believe in him through

the testimony of his first disciples in John 17 and calls "blessed" we who have "not seen and yet believe" in John 20.

The point is that we are to see ourselves at sea and mountain, at cross and tomb *in a way more real than historical.* Year by year we rehearse the events of Jesus' birth, ministry, suffering, death, resurrection, ascension, and gift of the Spirit – all so that we might know and believe more truly that Jesus literally was bearing our sins on the cross (because we were there) and that he was raised for our justification (because we were there, too).

Therefore, to change the point of reference from biblical times to the present day, in our baptisms we believe that we truly are buried and raised with Christ (because we were there), and we receive from Christ's own hand his body and his blood, "given and shed for you" (because we were there, too). The Great Commission to "go and make disciples of all nations" rings in our own ears, as do our Lord's words and examples of passionate concern for the hungry, the needy, those cast out, and the outsiders in our midst.

Finally, then, we can live in view of the end promised in the Bible's final book, as celebrated on the church year's final Sunday, Christ the King, as we anticipate and already rejoice in God's making all things right and new, even in a world where we know this to be true by faith and not by sight.

The Season of Advent

We begin, then, with the season in which our lips pray with the church of all ages: "*Maranatha!* (Our Lord, come!)" (1 Cor 16:22 see also Rev 22:20). "Advent" (Latin for "coming-to") refers to Jesus' coming in history, mystery, and majesty, that is, as a human in the first century of our era, in present reality through Word and Sacrament and in our neighbor in need, and in glory as victorious Lord of time and eternity.

Rejoice greatly, O daughter Zion!
  Shout aloud, O daughter Jerusalem!
Lo, your king comes to you;
  triumphant and victorious is he,
humble and riding on a donkey,
  on a colt, the foal of a donkey.
He will cut off the chariot from Ephraim
  and the war-horse from Jerusalem;
and the battle bow shall be cut off,
  and he shall command peace to the nations;
his dominion shall be from sea to sea,
  and from the River to the ends of the earth.
                                    (Zechariah 9:9-10)

God,

We are not patient people. Help us to wait faithfully. Even more, help us to know and welcome you when you are present among us, that we may be most truly ready when you come in glory as Lord and Love of all. Amen!

Christmas Day
(25 December)

The Christian celebration of Christmas has a two-fold focus: the story of what happened and what the story means. Without the story there is, of course, no meaning, but without consideration of the meaning, the story devolves into sentimentality and cuteness, leading to oft-remarked abuses of the "season."

Jesus was literally Anselm of Canterbury's definition of God: "than which none greater can be conceived" (although Anselm meant "thought of"). But conceived he was, and born, for the explicit purpose of defeating death by dying, saving God's people from their sins, and exampling human life in all its God-willed fullness.

And she gave birth to her firstborn son and wrapped him in bands of cloth, and laid him in a manger, because there was no place for them in the inn.
(Luke 2:7)

In the beginning was the Word, and the Word was with God, and the Word was God. . . . And the Word became flesh and lived among us, and we have seen his glory, the glory as of a father's only son, full of grace and truth.
(John 1:1, 14)

O God,

Who hast caused this holy night to shine with the illumination of the true Light: Grant us, we beseech thee, that as we have known the mystery of that Light upon earth, so may we also perfectly enjoy him in heaven; where with thee and the Holy Spirit he liveth and reigneth, one God, in glory everlasting. Amen!
(Thomas Cranmer [1489-1556])

147

The Twelve Days of Christmas
(25 December – 5 January)

Traditionally, the days between Christmas and Epiphany have been observed as an on-going celebration of Christmas (as best known through the famous, if utterly secular, "partridge in a pear tree" song). But from a Christian perspective, these days can be much more.

The very structure of the church year reminds us that the pattern that Jesus set of attaining glory through submission and suffering obtains for his followers. Each of the first three days following Christmas celebrates before God an individual or group whose association with Jesus entailed a heavy price: St. Stephen, martyr (the 26th); St. John, evangelist (the 27th); and the Innocents of Bethlehem (the 28th). Further, on New Year's Day the church year recalls Jesus' naming ("Savior") and his full participation as one of the covenant people of God through his circumcision.

The point of these reflections is not to dampen our celebration but to enrich it, by recalling the stakes in play for Jesus and for those who bear his name from the very moment of his birth and of our birth in him.

If any want to become my followers, let them deny themselves and take up their cross and follow me. (Mark 8:34)

We thank you, God,

For this time of recess and rejoicing. As we celebrate and refresh, give us the maturity and perspective to find our pleasure and peace in your service – any price. In the name of him whose name we bear, Jesus Christ our Lord. Amen!

The Season of the Epiphany

The Christmas-centric portion of the church year begins with the preparation time of Advent, climaxes in the celebration of Jesus' birth at Christmas, and concludes with the Epiphany season.

"Epiphany" means "showing forth" and, like Christmas itself, has two foci. One is a stress on the events of Jesus' ministry before his passion and death, known from the Gospel accounts of what Jesus said and did largely in his home region of Galilee. The other emphasis of the season picks up on the theme of Galilee – the most ethnically diverse region in the Holy Land of Jesus' time – as we recall that Jesus was "a light for revelation to the Gentiles," as well as "for glory to your people Israel" (Luke 2:32). Otherwise put, Epiphany is the church year's mission time, encouraging us to "show forth" Jesus to the whole world, beginning with whatever place (or "Galilee") we call home.

Arise, shine; for your light has come, and the glory of the LORD has risen upon you. For darkness shall cover the earth, and thick darkness the peoples; but the LORD will arise upon you, and his glory will appear over you. Nations shall come to your light, and kings to the brightness of your dawn. (Isaiah 60:1-3)

Lord God,

We live in a time of great and growing diversity. Enable us to bear winsome witness in what we say and do to the light that your Son has brought to our lives and world. Help us to embrace those who are "other" to us and to treat them with the respect due to those of your own making and redeeming. Let our lives join our words as praise and proclamation, in Jesus' name. Amen!

The Day of the Epiphany
(6 January)

Most often, when we think of Christian missions, we have in mind efforts to go forth to the ends of the earth. This conception is not wrong (as witnessed by the Acts of the Apostles), but it is neither the first nor the only model. The Old Testament speaks more often of the nations coming to God's "light" in Jerusalem (as in Isaiah 60). Similarly, Matthew's account of the birth of the Christ describes the pilgrimage of magi from the "East" to worship the child in his birthplace, Bethlehem (a mere five miles south of Jerusalem).

Yet whatever the direction of travel – whether the Gospel is taken to others or draws others to its light – the magi's question to the inhabitants of Jerusalem, "Where is the King of the Jews?," cautions us that the values and structures of those who already stand in God's promises require as much critical review as of those who do not yet know him.

When [the wise men] saw that the star had stopped, they were overwhelmed with joy. On entering the house, they saw the child with Mary his mother; and they knelt down and paid him homage. Then, opening their treasure chests, they offered him gifts of gold, frankincense, and myrrh. (Matthew 2:10-11)

Make us wise, O God,

And draw us to you, just as once you pulled wise men by a star, and just as once Jesus promised that, when he was lifted up from the earth, he would draw all people to himself. Enable us to shed every weight and distraction, and let our witness serve also to attract others. In Jesus' name. Amen!

The Baptism of our Lord
(The First Sunday after the Epiphany
and the Remembrance of Our Own Baptismal Birthday)

In addition to its emphasis upon Jesus as "light to the nations," the Epiphany season recalls the words and events of Jesus' ministry before its final week of passion and death. That ministry was literally inaugurated with Jesus' baptism, in which God testified that Jesus was both his royal Son and his soon-to-be-suffering servant, as the voice melded two key Old Testament passages. Particularly Mark's Gospel reminds us that baptism – including ours – is part of our daily dying and rising with Christ.

I will tell of the decree of the LORD: He said to me, "You are my son; today I have begotten you." (Psalm 2:7)

Here is my servant, whom I uphold, my chosen, in whom my soul delights…. (Isaiah 42:1a)

In those days Jesus came from Nazareth of Galilee and was baptized by John in the Jordan. And just as he was coming up out of the water, he saw the heavens torn apart and the Spirit descending like a dove on him. And a voice came from heaven, "You are my Son, the Beloved; with you I am well pleased." (Mark 1:9-11)

The cup that I drink you will drink; and with the baptism with which I am baptized, you will be baptized…. (Mark 10:39b)

Lord God,

Remind me daily of my baptism, in which I "put on Christ," and enable me day-by-day to "walk in newness of life." In his name. Amen!

Week of Prayer for Christian Unity
(18-25 January)

Within the Epiphany season fall two special commemorations: the Confession of St. Peter on 18 January and the Conversion of St. Paul on the 25th. These two days emphasize the grace that God showed in leading the chief apostles to Israel and to the Gentiles, respectively (Galatians 2:7-8), to faith in Jesus as Messiah and Lord (Peter in Matthew 16:17 and Paul in Acts 9).

The intervening week raises a stark contrast, therefore, between Jesus' expressed desire for oneness (not sameness) among his followers and the fragmentation present since New Testament times. We pray always – but with special fervor in this week – that "our sad divisions soon will cease" and that our Gospel witness will be enhanced by unity in the church's confession of Jesus as Christ and Lord.

I ask not only on behalf of these [original disciples], but also on behalf of those who will believe in me through their word, that they may all be one. As you, Father, are in me and I am in you, may they also be in us, so that the world may believe that you have sent me.
(John 17:20-21)

For all your church on earth, we intercede; Lord, make our sad divisions soon to cease; draw us all closer, each to each, we plead, by drawing all to you, O Prince of Peace; thus may we all one bread, one body be, through this blest Sacrament of unity. Amen!
(William H. Turton [1856-1938])

The Transfiguration of our Lord
(The Last Sunday after the Epiphany)

The Epiphany season began with the magi's pilgrimage and the initiation of Jesus' public ministry with his baptism. It concludes as Jesus "sets his face" to go up to Jerusalem (Luke 9:51). Once again, the voice proclaims Jesus as Son and servant. Moses and Elijah – themselves no strangers to encounters with God on mountains – discuss with Jesus the "departure [Gk. *exodus*], which he was about to accomplish at Jerusalem" (Luke 9:31). All the while, Jesus stands "transfigured," anticipating both Easter and the final exodus/Easter of the book of Revelation.

All about is "glory," the cloud that had enveloped the tabernacle in the wilderness long ago, in which God had "epiphanied" his presence in the midst of his people, Israel. In both the afterglow and anticipation of God's glory, we enter the shadows of Lent this Wednesday.

Now the appearance of the glory of the LORD was like a devouring fire on the top of the mountain in the sight of the people of Israel. Moses entered the cloud, and went up on the mountain.

(Exodus 24:17-18a)

Blessed are you, O Lord our God, king of the universe, who led your people Israel by a pillar of cloud by day and a pillar of fire by night: Enlighten our darkness by the light of your Christ; may his Word be a lamp to our feet and a light to our path; for you are merciful, and you love your whole creation, and we, your creatures, glorify you, Father, Son, and Holy Spirit. Amen!

(*Lutheran Book of Worship*, Evening Prayer:Vespers)

The Season of Lent

Those who grew up observing the church year naturally connect Lent with somber hymns and prolonged focus on our sin and Jesus' death. But such associations may impoverish our use of Lent. The word "Lent" comes from the Old English for "springtime"; it first served as a time of instructing new Christians, in preparation for their baptism at the Easter Vigil. Lent reminds us that part of our life's journey is growth in the content of our faith, a process that necessarily has an intellectual component.

In fact, more than any other season of the church year, Lent is well-considered as a journey. Its forty days remind us of Israel's forty years of preparation for the Promised Land, as well as Jesus' forty days in the desert following his baptism, as he considered alternatives to dying on a cross. In addition, Luke's Gospel, especially, depicts Jesus' journey to Jerusalem, where he would work his "exodus."

If any want to become my followers, let them deny themselves and take up their cross daily and follow me. For those who want to save their life will lose it, and those who lose their life for my sake will save it.
(Luke 9:23-24)

Lord Jesus, pioneer and perfecter of our faith,

Help us to follow you as we journey through Lent and through life. In good times, keep us from complacency, and give us the discipline to worship you with our minds. In hard times, keep us from despair, reminding us always that we *follow* you with our crosses, because you have borne yours ahead of us. At all times, stay our steps, and stay with us. Amen!

Ash Wednesday

According to Leviticus 16, once each year Israel
was to assemble before God, repent of its sins – known and
unknown, intentional and accidental – and receive atonement.
Christianity's closest analog to the Day of Atonement is not so
much Good Friday as Ash Wednesday, the first day of Lent. It
is especially on Ash Wednesday that we gather before God to
acknowledge how far short of God's intentions we have fallen
and how utterly dependent we are on God's grace for hope of
forgiveness and renewal of life.

> *Yet even now, says the LORD,*
> *return to me with all your heart,*
> *with fasting, with weeping, and with mourning;*
> *rend your hearts and not your clothing.*
> *Return to the LORD, your God,*
> *for he is gracious and merciful,*
> *slow to anger, and abounding in steadfast love,*
> *and relents from punishing.*
> (Joel 2:12-13)

God,

We simply have no alternative: we throw ourselves on your
mercy. We cannot get through a day – not even an hour –
without betraying the trust and honor that you placed in us,
when you first made humanity in your image. We can put up
a good front sometimes, but deep down inside we know that we
neither love you with all our being nor our neighbor as ourselves.
For all our sins and failures we come to you for pardon. Grant us
your peace, provide us grace to forgive as we have been forgiven,
and create in us clean hearts. We pray in Jesus' name. Amen!

The Annunciation of our Lord
(25 March)

The celebration of Jesus' birth on the 25th of December was
an arbitrary choice by the early church. Christians probably
co-opted the Roman festival of the Birth of the Invincible Sun,
which followed soon after the winter solstice. First, then, this day
is an affirmation of Jesus' fully human nature: his conception is
calculated at exactly nine months prior to his birth.

But there are numerous other facets to this day. Mary serves as
a model of straight talk with God ("How can this be?"), of faith
in God's promises (even when absurd), and of embracing God's
call – or vocation ("Let it be to me according to your word").
Moreover, the occurrence of this day in the midst of Lent is one
more reminder that the babe of Bethlehem was under the shadow
of the cross from the moment of his conception.

But when the fullness of time had come, God sent his Son, born of a
woman, born under the law, in order to redeem those who were under
the law, so that we might receive adoption as children.

(Galatians 4:4-5)

Lord God,

Your engagement with your physical creation has been a marvel
for us humans from the moment you first set hand to dust.
But how far beyond that is your choice to enter our clay yourself.
Your incarnation grants infinite dignity to every person. Let us
live as those so honored and treat others with like regard. In Jesus'
name. Amen!

The Sunday of the Passion
(Palm Sunday)

This day begins what has long been called "Holy Week" – an apt name, especially given that "holy" means, at its core, "set apart." If God's plan of salvation is conceived of as a drama, then this week marks its climax, an assessment supported by the centrality given to the events that we recall this week in all four Gospels. It is time set apart within all history.

Today, like several others that we have described, has two foci. The traditional emphasis is on Jesus' entry into Jerusalem, or "Palm Sunday." The second, newer emphasis is upon the entire story of his passion. The "triumphal entry" is thereby set in perspective: there is no way to glory except via the cross, the way of self-sacrifice, humiliation, even death.

Let the same mind be in you that was in Christ Jesus, who, though he was in the form of God, did not regard equality with God as something to be exploited, but emptied himself, taking the form of a slave, being born in human likeness. And being found in human form, he humbled himself and became obedient to the point of death – even death on a cross. Therefore God also highly exalted him and gave him the name that is above every name, so that at the name of Jesus every knee should bend, in heaven and on earth and under the earth, and every tongue confess that Jesus Christ is Lord, to the glory of God the Father. (Philippians 2:5-11)

Lord Jesus Christ, you gave up everything for our sakes. Move not merely our knees and our tongues but our whole lives, that they may befit those who bear your name and bear winsome witness to your way of glorifying God. Amen!

157

Maundy Thursday

This day takes its name from Jesus' words in John 13:34a:
"I give you a new commandment [Latin: *mandatum novum*],
that you love one another." What Jesus had in mind by that "new
commandment" he had just illustrated by a slave's work, washing
his disciples' feet. Still, the chief emphasis for most Christians is
on the gift of the Lord's Supper, recounted in every Gospel *except*
John. It is St. Paul who brings together meal and mandate:

*The cup of blessing that we bless, is it not a sharing in the blood
of Christ? The bread that we break, is it not a sharing in the body
of Christ? Because there is one bread, we who are many are one body,
for we all partake of the one bread.* (1 Corinthians 10:16-17)

In the Lord's Supper we individually receive the body and blood
of Christ for the forgiveness of our sins (Matt 26:26-28). But we
who receive Christ's body *are* Christ's body. We who make up the
body of Christ are most fully visible as that one body when we act
least according to our innate, individual interest, that is, when we
"love one another."

Lord God,

In a wonderful Sacrament you have left us a memorial of your
suffering and death. May this Sacrament of your body and blood
so work in us that the way we live will proclaim the redemption
you have brought; for you live and reign with the Father and the
Holy Spirit, one God, now and forever. Amen!

(Thomas Aquinas [c1225-1274])

Good Friday

This is the second of the "Great Three Days"
(or *Triduum*), and in this day's events God's plan of salvation
comes to its awful, awe-full climax. As Mary says in a play by
Dorothy Sayers: "This is reality. From the beginning of time
until now, this is the only thing that has ever really happened."
(*The Man Born to be King*, 1943:289)

Each of the four Gospels features a distinct, complementary
perspective. For Matthew, Jesus is the goat of Yom Kippur who
dies for sin. For Mark, Jesus suffers alone and abandoned even
by God (15:34), literally experiencing hell. Luke's Jesus dies
with words of blessing on his lips for his friends, his enemies,
and a stranger, before giving himself into his Father's keeping
with a child's prayer (23:28-31, 34, 43, 46). In John, Jesus dies
as *the* Passover lamb, draws all people to himself (12:32), and
is enthroned as king of the universe, with history's shortest
inaugural address: *"It is finished"* (19:30). Taken together, the
Gospels provide a three-dimensional portrait that addresses "all
sorts and conditions of people."

*When I came to you, brothers and sisters, I did not come proclaiming
the mystery of God to you in lofty words and phrases. For I decided
to know nothing among you except Jesus Christ, and him crucified.*
(1 Corinthians 2:1-2)

Lord Christ,

On the cross you suffered in our place, showed us how to live and
die, and proved yourself Victor King over death and evil. Draw us
to you, above all this day, just as you promised. Amen!

The Vigil of Easter

"Why is this night different from all other nights?" This question begins the great narrative of the Jewish Passover Seder, recounting God's mighty deliverance of Israel from bondage in Egypt. For Christians *this* is the night that is different from all other nights, because, as the ancient Vigil liturgy has it: "This is the night in which, breaking the chains of death, Christ arises from hell in triumph."

The Vigil of Easter includes numerous themes. New fire is struck and the paschal candle is lighted, marking Christ's pass-over from death to life (Gk. *pascha*, "Easter"). A series of Old Testament readings recounts the mighty acts of our Creator and Redeemer, pointing us in sum to Easter, the first day of the new creation. Baptisms are performed and recalled, reconnecting us with the crossing of the sea in Exodus and reminding us that baptism is Easter made personal. Finally, the Eucharist is celebrated, in which the risen Christ appears to us as to the first disciples and in which we look forward to an Easter that will not end.

For our paschal lamb, Christ, has been sacrificed. Therefore, let us celebrate the festival, not with the old yeast, the yeast of malice and evil, but with the unleavened bread of sincerity and truth.

(1 Corinthians 5:7b-8

O Lord,

Let no repetition of the news of this night dull our marvel or our joy, as we take in all that it means that death is not the end, but only birth to new and fuller life in you. Let us live, then, "as newborn babes, desiring the sincere milk of the Word." In Jesus' name. Amen!

The Resurrection of our Lord
(Easter Day)

The day started ordinarily enough. Women made their way quietly, in the early morning hours, to do what women did in those days, to do right as could be done by those whom death had done wrong. Their minds were focused, practical: "Who will roll away the stone?"

As things turned out, that question was irrelevant. So were the spices that they had brought. So was the purpose for which they had come. As time went by, there were different memories of exactly who had said what to whom, but the upshot was clear enough. No fear! No corpse! Come see! Go tell!

To this day, that's the nub of the Easter Gospel.

When they looked up, they saw that the stone, which was very large, had already been rolled back. As they entered the tomb, they saw a young man, dressed in a white robe, sitting on the right side; and they were alarmed. But he said to them, "Do not be alarmed; you are looking for Jesus of Nazareth, who was crucified. He has been raised; he is not here. Look, there is the place they laid him. But go, tell his disciples and Peter that he is going ahead of you to Galilee; there you will see him, just as he told you."
(Mark 16:4-7)

Hail thee, festival day! Blest day to be hallowed forever; day when our Lord was raised, breaking the kingdom of death.
(Venantius Honorius Fortunatus [c530-609])

161

Ascension Day

According to Acts 1:3, Jesus "presented himself alive to them by many convincing proofs, appearing to them *during forty days* and speaking about the kingdom of God." It is therefore on the fortieth day after Easter that the church year observes the departure of his physical presence.

What is the significance of the ascension of Jesus? Christian creeds affirm that Jesus was thereby "seated at the right hand of the Father." But the Bible stresses more its benefits for us:

Do not let your hearts be troubled. Believe in God, believe also in me. In my Father's house are many dwelling places. If it were not so, would I have told you that I go to prepare a place for you?
(John 14:1-2)

But each of us was given grace according to the measure of Christ's gif̃ Therefore it is said, "When he ascended on high he made captivity itself a captive; he gave gifts to his people." (Ephesians 4:7-̃)

And Jesus' final words in Matthew's Gospel (28:20b) add an important assurance:

"And remember, I am with you always, to the end of the age."

Lord Jesus,

You once told Thomas, "Blessed are those who have not seen [me] and yet have come to believe." Lord, we believe; help our unbelief. Amen!

The Day of Pentecost

Like Passover, Pentecost was in the first place a
Jewish festival. Its name comes from Greek-speaking Diaspora
Jews. The Old Testament calls it the Festival of Weeks or the
Festival of Harvest. Because it is celebrated fifty days after
Passover, it came to be called Pentecost (as in Greek *pente*, "five").
Thus, not to belabor the obvious, all of those people were in
Jerusalem in Acts 2 to celebrate the Jewish Pentecost, not the
Christian one!

But God's selection of this festival day for the gift of the Holy
Spirit is more than coincidental. Pentecost celebrated the new
harvest in the spring of the year. On this day, then, a new harvest
of a different sort began, as tongues *of* fire yielded tongues *on* fire,
speaking in the tongues of all, and the "Jesus movement" began its
spread "in Jerusalem, in all Judea and Samaria, and to the ends of
the earth."

(Acts 1:8)

*In the last days it will be, God declares, that I will pour out my
Spirit upon all flesh, and your sons and your daughters shall prophesy,
and your young men shall see visions, and your old men shall dream
dreams. Even upon my slaves, both men and women, in those days I
will pour out my Spirit; and they shall prophesy.*

(Acts 2:17-18, quoting Joel 2:28-29)

Come, Holy Ghost, Creator blest,
And make our hearts your place of rest;
Come with your grace and heav'nly aid,
And fill the hearts which you have made. Amen!

(Rabanus Maurus [c780-856])

The Holy Trinity
(The First Sunday after Pentecost)

"I baptize you in the name of the Father and of the Son and of the Holy Spirit" – these words quote the "Great Commission" of Jesus in Matthew 28:19, as he details one of two crucial elements in making disciples of all nations (the other is teaching). Thus, while neither Jesus nor any writer in the New Testament employs the word "Trinity," we do learn from Scripture that the Christian God has a name.

Exactly what that name *means* and tells us about God has been the subject of extensive debate. That issue, along with what it means to affirm Jesus' full humanity and divinity, led finally to the councils that defined orthodox Christianity.

There's no denying that what we believe and teach about the Trinity and Jesus is important and has consequences. (The Athanasian Creed goes so far as to say: "This is the catholic faith. One cannot be saved without believing this firmly and faithfully.") Yet the focus of this day is not the celebration of a doctrine, but rather the *praise* of the God whose self-revelation to us is as Father, Son, and Spirit. God's work among us is a function of God's own nature. For that we are thankful – naturally.

The grace of our Lord Jesus Christ, the love of God, and the communion of the Holy Spirit be with all of you.

(2 Corinthians 13:13)

Thank you, God, for being as you are, so that we might hope to be as you would have us. In Jesus' name. Amen!

The Ordinary Time of the Church
(The Season after Pentecost)

For half a year we have reheard and relived the axial events of the life and work of Jesus. But life goes on – in fact, thanks to Jesus, life goes on and on. The second half of the church year is an extended answer to "So what?": So what that Jesus was born, lived, died, and rose again? What does it mean for us who live between those events and the final consummation that we celebrate on Christ the King Sunday?

The coming months affirm, first of all, that we live in the aftermath of Pentecost; that is, we are a people "on the way" (see Acts 9:2). At the same time, we are the body of Christ, whose very breath is the Spirit of God. We are the visible presence of Christ: his voice; his eyes; his hands; his feet. As such, we "proclaim the good news of God" (Mark 1:14), trusting in God to give growth to us and to our work.

> *For as the rain and the snow come down from heaven,*
> *and do not return there until they have watered the earth,*
> *making it bring forth and sprout,*
> *giving seed to the sower and bread to the eater,*
> *so shall my word be that goes out from my mouth;*
> *it shall not return to me empty,*
> *but it shall accomplish that which I purpose,*
> *and succeed in the thing for which I sent it.*
> (Isaiah 55:10-11)

Heavenly Father,

You have made us your people. Be with us in our becoming, even as you brought us into being. Bless all that we do and all whom we serve in Jesus' name. Amen!

Holy Cross Day
(14 September)

For decades, Valparaiso University has described itself as a "university under the cross." It is therefore appropriate that the VU community should take special note of this day as a reminder of our distinctive mission, especially as the observance comes so early in each new academic year.

For a Lutheran Christian university, the day has special significance because of the centrality of Luther's "theology of the cross," that we know God most completely in Christ crucified. Such a theology reminds us that, as humans, we are never in full possession of the truth, fully expressed for all times and places, and that all pretensions to such knowledge must be left at the cross, along with every other human presumption. Our community's academic mission is thereby informed by its spiritual foundation, and our search for truth is thereby both inspired and humbled.

Now is the judgment of this world; now the ruler of this world will be driven out. And I, when I am lifted up from the earth, will draw all people to myself.   (John 12:31-32)

But we proclaim Christ crucified, a stumbling block to Jews and foolishness to Gentiles, but to those who are the called, both Jews and Greeks, Christ the power of God and the wisdom of God.
(1 Corinthians 1:23-24)

Help us to live and learn "under the cross," Lord God, for it is there that we can best know your own mind and heart. Amen!

Reformation Day
(31 October)

Valparaiso University is a Lutheran Christian university,
so it is appropriate to observe the one day of the church year that
is particularly Lutheran. At the same time, it would be a
fundamental betrayal of Luther's theology of the cross to make
this as an occasion for triumphalism. Rather, the proper focus
of this day is on the praise of God in Christ.

Specifically, we praise God for reminding the church that at
the heart of the Christian Gospel lies a God who spared nothing
to rescue a humanity so alienated from God that we could do
nothing on our own behalf.

Twentieth-century American comedian Groucho Marx once
said, "I don't care to belong to a club that accepts people like
me as members." The wonder is that God not only wants us as
members of his Church: he sent his Son to die, so that we might
do so without price.

*For God so loved the world that he gave his only Son, so that everyone
who believes in him may not perish but may have eternal life. Indeed,
God did not send the Son into the world to condemn the world, but in
order that the world might be saved through him.*   (John 3:16-17)

Dear God,

Your justice is awesome and your mercy more awesome still.
Strengthen our trust in your promises of forgiveness and life for
Jesus' sake, and enable us to give freely, as we have freely received.
Amen!

All Saints' Day
(1 November)

During the Great Thanksgiving in the liturgy, the presiding minister says: "and so, with all the choirs of angels, with the church on earth and the hosts of heaven, we praise your name and join their unending hymn." Who are these "hosts of heaven"? All Saints' Day reminds us that we are but the most recent of a long line of those who have borne the name of Christ. In our worship we join our voices with theirs.

In addition, while the church year includes numerous commemorations of extraordinary individuals, All Saints' Day recalls for us that every individual member of the Body of Christ is precious. What counts is not status, success, or fame, but faithfulness to our calling and to our Lord.

Then one of the elders addressed me, saying, "Who are these, robed in white, and where have they come from?" I said to him, "Sir, you are the one who knows." Then he said to me, "These are they who have come out of the great ordeal; they have washed their robes and made them white in the blood of the Lamb.

For this reason they are before the throne of God,
and worship him day and night within his temple,
and the one who is seated on the throne will shelter them."

(Revelation 7:13-15)

Lord God, join our prayers and praises with those of your servants of every time and every place, and unite them with the ceaseless petitions of our great high priest until he comes as victorious Lord of all. Amen! (*Lutheran Book of Worship*, Eucharistic Prayer)

Christ the King Sunday
(The Last Sunday after Pentecost)

For the Christian, life is not just one thing after another, or an endless cycle and then you die. Life has a goal, an endpoint that is not the end. Today we both look forward to that goal and celebrate its presence already among us.

The goal was announced by both John the Baptist and Jesus: "The kingdom of God has come near" (Matthew 3:2; Mark 1:15). God's rule is real, even if not fully and obviously apparent – yet. History has passed a tipping point, and although serious struggle remains, the outcome is not in doubt. Already we can join with the Psalmist: "Say among the nations, 'The LORD is king!'" (Psalm 96:10).

As I watched in the night visions,
  I saw one like a human being coming with the clouds of heaven.
  And he came to the Ancient One and was presented before him.
  To him was given dominion and glory and kingship,
  that all peoples, nations, and languages should serve him.
  His dominion is an everlasting dominion that shall not pass away,
  and his kingship is one that shall never be destroyed.

(Daniel 7:13-14)

Lord God,

"Your kingdom come," we pray. Let your rule come and be known and praised – within ourselves, in our campus community, in our families and homes, and in our world. Let it come as Jesus brought it, as we serve humbly as your means of healing and hope, especially for those in desperate need of both. Your kingdom come, Lord, in grace and at the last in power. In the name of Jesus. Amen!

Promise

**For God alone
my soul waits
in silence;
from him
comes my salvation.**

PSALM 62:1

Purpose – Observing silence allows one to be receptive to God's voice. With an attitude of anticipation one waits for God to bring a life-giving word.

Practice – Silence has been highly prized as a Christian discipline through the ages because as one attends to God's voice, one's inner being becomes focused and intent on receiving life, blessing and spiritual richness from the One who is the source of life, blessing and wisdom.

Process

1. Find a place of solitude away from all distractions.

2. Use a candle, icon, picture or cross and make it your source of focus.

3. Quiet yourself by attending to your breathing.

4. Seek inner silence and begin to listen to God.

5. If your mind turns to inner chatter, take a full breath and calm yourself.

6. When ready, whisper a "Thank you, God" and turn to what or who needs your attention.

Prayer – Pray God to help you rid yourself of distraction so that you may know joy in the refuge of silence.

What is more pleasing than a psalm?

David expressed it well:
　"Praise the Lord, for a psalm is good:
　let there be praise of our God
　with gladness and grace!"

Yes, a psalm is
　a blessing on the lips of the people,
　praise of God,
　the assembly's homage,
　a general acclamation,
　a word that speaks for all,
　the voice of the Church,
　a confession of faith in song.
　　　　St. Ambrose of Milan (339-397)

When feeling insignificant – Psalm 8

O Lord, our Sovereign,
　how majestic is your name in all the earth!

You have set your glory above the heavens.
Out of the mouths of babes and infants
　you have founded a bulwark because of your foes,
　to silence the enemy and the avenger.

When I look at your heavens, the work of your fingers,
　the moon and the stars that you have established;
　what are human beings that you are mindful of them,
　mortals that you care for them?

Yet you have made them a little lower than God,
　and crowned them with glory and honor.
You have given them dominion
　over the works of your hands;
　you have put all things under their feet,
　all sheep and oxen and also the beasts of the field,

the birds of the air, and the fish of the sea,
whatever passes along the paths of the seas.

O Lord, our Sovereign,
how majestic is your name in all the earth!

When lonely – Psalm 23

The Lord is my shepherd, I shall not want.
He makes me lie down in green pastures;
he leads me beside still waters;
he restores my soul,
He leads me in right paths for his name's sake.

Even though I walk through the darkest valley,
I fear no evil;
for you are with me;
your rod and your staff – they comfort me.

You prepare a table before me
in the presence of my enemies;
you anoint my head with oil;
my cup overflows.
Surely goodness and mercy shall follow me
all the days of my life,
and I shall dwell in the house of the Lord
my whole life long.

When seeking God's light – Psalm 36:7-9

How precious is your steadfast love, O God!
All people may take refuge in the shadow of your wings.
They feast on the abundance of your house,
and you give them drink from
the river of your delights.
For with you is the fountain of life;
in your light we see light.

173

When thanking God – Psalm 30:1-5, 11-12

I will extol you, O Lord, for you have drawn me up,
   and did not let my foes rejoice over me.
O Lord my God, I cried to you for help,
   and you have healed me.
O Lord, you brought up my soul from Sheol,
   restored me to life from among those
   gone down to the Pit.

Sing praises to the Lord, O you his faithful ones,
   and give thanks to his holy name.
For his anger is but for a moment;
   his favor is for a lifetime.
Weeping may linger for the night,
   but joy comes with the morning.

You have turned my mourning into dancing;
   you have taken off my sackcloth
   and clothed me with joy,
so that my soul may praise you and not be silent.
   O Lord my God, I will give thanks to you forever.

When sick, suffering – Psalm 103:1-5

Bless the Lord, O my soul, and all that is within me,
   bless his holy name.
Bless the Lord, O my soul, and do not forget all his
   benefits –
who forgives all your iniquity,
   who heals all your diseases,
who redeems your life from the Pit,
   who crowns you with steadfast love and mercy,
who satisfies you with good as long as you live
   so that your youth is renewed like the eagle's.

TAKING OUR CARES TO THE LIGHT
Spoken in the Psalms, which give Light

I AM the Good Shepherd.
John 10:11

When feeling attacked – Psalm 70

Be pleased, O God, to deliver me.
  O Lord, make haste to help me!
Let those be put to shame and confusion
  who seek my life.
Let those be turned back and brought to dishonor
  who desire to hurt me.
Let those who say, "Aha, Aha!" turn back
  because of their shame.

Let all who seek you rejoice and be glad in you.
Let those who love your salvation say evermore,
  "God is great!"
But I am poor and needy; hasten to me, O God!
You are my help and my deliverer;
  O Lord, do not delay!

When hungering for assurance – Psalm 118:1-9

O give thanks to the Lord, for he is good;
  his steadfast love endures forever!
Let Israel say, "His steadfast love endures forever."
Let the house of Aaron say, "His steadfast love
  endures forever."
Let those who fear the Lord say, "His steadfast love
  endures forever."

Out of my distress I called on the Lord;
  the Lord answered me and set me in a broad place.
With the Lord on my side I do not fear.
  What can mortals do to me?
The Lord is on my side to help me;
  I shall look in triumph on those who hate me.
It is better to take refuge in the Lord
  than to put confidence in mortals.
It is better to take refuge in the Lord
  than to put confidence in princes.

When unsure where to look for help – Psalm 121

I lift up my eyes to the hills –
from where will my help come?
My help comes from the Lord,
who made heaven and earth.

He will not let your foot be moved;
he who keeps you will not slumber.
He who keeps Israel will neither slumber nor sleep.

The Lord is your keeper;
the Lord is your shade at your right hand.
The sun shall not strike you by day,
nor the moon by night.

The Lord will keep you from all evil;
he will keep your life.
The Lord will keep your going out and your coming in
from this time on and forevermore.

When wishing to praise God – Psalm 150

Praise the Lord! Praise God in his sanctuary;
praise him in his mighty firmament!
Praise him for his mighty deeds;
praise him according to his surpassing greatness!

Praise him with trumpet sound;
praise him with lute and harp!
Praise him with tambourine and dance;
praise him with strings and pipe!
Praise him with clanging cymbals;
praise him with loud clashing cymbals!
Let everything that breathes praise the Lord!
Praise the Lord!

TAKING OUR CARES TO THE LIGHT
Spoken by Jesus, the Light

The Lord's Prayer
Translated in English, German, and Spanish

Our Father in heaven,
Vater unser im Himmel,
Padre nuestro, que estás en el cielo
> **hallowed be your name.**
> *geheiligt werde dein Name.*
> *Santificado sea Tu nombre;*

Your kingdom come.
Dein Reich komme.
Venga a nosotros Tu reino.
> **Your will be done,**
> *Dein Wille geschehe,*
> *Hágase Tu voluntad*

on earth as it is in heaven.
wie im Himmel so auf Erden.
En la tierra como en el cielo.
> **Give us this day our daily bread.**
> *Unser tägliches Brot gib uns heute.*
> *Danos hoy nuestro pan de cada día.*

And forgive us our debts,
Und vergib uns unsere Schuld,
Perdona nuestras ofensas,
> **as we also have forgiven our debtors.**
> *wie auch wir vergeben unsern Schuldigern.*
> *Como también nosotros perdonamos a los que nos ofenden.*

And do not bring us to the time of trial,
Und führe uns nicht in Versuchung,
Y no nos dejes caer en la tentación;
> **but rescue us from the evil one.**
> *sondern erlöse uns von dem Bösen.*
> *libranos de todo mal.*

For the kingdom, the power, and the glory are yours,
Denn dein ist das Reich und die Kraft und die Herrlichkeit
Porque Tuyo es el Reino, el Poder y la Gloria
> **Now and forever. Amen.**
> *In Ewigkeit. Amen.*
> *por siempre, Señor. Amén.*

(Matthew 6:9-13)

Rejoicing at the return of the 70

At that same hour Jesus rejoiced in the Holy Spirit and said, *I thank you, Father, Lord of heaven and earth, because you have hidden these things from the wise and the intelligent and have revealed them to infants; yes, Father, for such was your gracious will.* (Luke 10:21-22)

At the tomb of Lazarus

So they took away the stone. And Jesus looked upward and said, *Father, I thank you for having heard me. I knew that you always hear me, but I have said this for the sake of the crowd standing here, so that they may believe that you sent me.* When he had said this, he cried with a loud voice, *Lazarus, come out!* (John 11:41-43)

Giving thanks with disciples on Maundy Thursday

Then he took a cup, and after giving thanks he said, *Take this and divide it among yourselves; for I tell you that from now on I will not drink of the fruit of the vine until the kingdom of God comes.*
(Luke 22:17-18)

In the Garden of Gethsemane

Then Jesus went with them to a place called Gethsemane; and he said to his disciples, *Sit here while I go over there and pray.* And going a little farther, he threw himself on the ground and prayed, *My Father, if it is possible, let this cup pass from me; yet not what I want but what you want.*

… Again he went away for the second time and prayed, *My Father, if this cannot pass unless I drink it, your will be done.*
(Matthew 26:36-39, 42)

TAKING OUR CARES TO THE LIGHT
Spoken by Jesus, the Light

On the Cross

Then Jesus said, *Father, forgive them; for they do not know what they are doing.* And they cast lots to divide his clothing. (Luke 23:34)

Just before His death

When it was noon, darkness came over the whole land until three in the afternoon. At three o'clock Jesus cried out with a loud voice, *Eloi, Eloi, lema sabachthani?* which means, *My God, my God, why have you forsaken me?* (Mark 15:33-34)

Asking the Father to be with his followers

After Jesus had spoken these words, he looked up to heaven and said, *Father, the hour has come; glorify your Son so that the Son may glorify you, since you have given him authority over all people, to give eternal life to all whom you have given him. And this is eternal life, that they may know you, the only true God, and Jesus Christ whom you have sent.*

. . Now they know that everything you have given me is from you; for the words that you gave to me I have given to them, and they have received them and know in truth that I came from you; and they have believed that you sent me.

. . Holy Father, protect them in your name that you have given me, so that they may be one, as we are one. While I was with them, I protected them in your name that you have given me.

. . But now I am coming to you, and I speak these things in the world so that they may have my joy made complete in themselves. I have given them your word, and the world has hated them because they do not belong to the world, just as I do not belong to the world. I am not asking you to take them out of the world, but I ask you to protect them from the evil one.

179

... I ask not only on behalf of those who will believe in me through their word, that they may all be one. As you, Father, are in me and I am in you, may they also be in us, so that the world may believe that you have sent me.

... Father, I desire that those also, whom you have given me, may be with me where I am, to see my glory, which you have given me because you loved me before the foundation of the world.

Righteous Father, the world does not know you, but I know you; and these know that you have sent me. I made your name known to them, and I will make it known, so that the love with which you have loved me may be in them, and I in them.

(John 17:1-3, 7-8, 11b-12a, 13-15, 20-21, 24-26)

> **"** There is no such thing as private
> or secret Christianity. Christians are called
> to personal faith, but never private faith. Christians
> are called not merely to believe in Jesus, but also
> to follow Him – to live as servants of God
> and others in community.
>
> *– Harry Wendt, author, teacher (1931-   )*
>
> I am not what I ought to be. I am not what
> I want to be. I am not what I hope to be.
> But still, I am not what I used to be.
> And by the grace of God, I am what I am.
>
> *– John Newton, clergyman, author*
> *(1725-1807)* **"**

TAKING OUR CARES TO THE LIGHT
Spoken by the Saints, who reflect the Light

I believe so that I may understand

I confess, Lord, with thanksgiving, that you have made me in your image, so that I can remember you, think of you, and love you.

But that image is so worn and blotted out by faults, and darkened by the smoke of sin, that it cannot do that for which it was made, unless you renew and refashion it.

Lord, I am not trying to make my way to your height, for my understanding is in no way equal to that, but I do desire to understand a little of your truth which my heart already believes and loves.

I do not seek to understand so that I can believe, but I believe so that I may understand; and what is more, I believe that unless I do believe, I shall not understand. Amen.

St. Anselm of Canterbury (1033-1109)

In your light may we see light clearly

Almighty and everlasting God, in whom we live and move and have our being, who has created us for yourself,

so that we can find rest only in you;

grant us purity of heart and strength of purpose,

that no selfish interest may hinder us from knowing your will, no weakness from doing it; but in your light may we see light clearly, and in your service find perfect freedom; through Jesus Christ our Lord. Amen.

St. Augustine, Bishop of Hippo (354-430)

To whom shall I cry?

O Lord, the house of my soul is narrow; enlarge it that thou mayest enter in. It is ruinous, O repair it! It displeases thy sight; I confess it, I know. But who shall cleanse it, or to whom shall I

cry but unto thee? Cleanse me from my secret faults, O Lord, and
spare thy servant from strange sins.

St. Augustine, Bishop of Hippo (354-430)

Wisdom to perceive you

O gracious and holy Father,
give us wisdom to perceive you,
intelligence to understand you,
diligence to seek you,
patience to wait for you,
eyes to behold you,
a heart to meditate upon you,
and a life to proclaim you,
through the power of the Spirit of our Lord Jesus Christ. Amen.

St. Benedict of Nursia (c.480-c.547)

God, come to our assistance

O Eternal Trinity, my sweet love!
You, light, give us light.
You, wisdom, give us wisdom,
You, supreme strength, strengthen us.
Today, eternal God, let our cloud be
dissipated so that we may perfectly know
and follow your Truth,
in truth, with a free and simple heart.
God, come to our assistance!
Lord, make haste to help us! Amen.

St. Catherine of Siena (1347-1380)

Make me an instrument of your peace

Lord, make me an instrument of your peace!

Where there is hatred, let me sow love;

where there is injury, pardon;
where there is doubt, faith;
where there is despair, hope;
where there is darkness, light;
and where there is sadness, joy.
O Divine Master,
grant that I may not
so much seek to be consoled as to console;
to be understood as to understand;
to be loved as to love;
for it is in giving that we receive;
it is in pardoning that we are pardoned;
and it is in dying that we are born to Eternal Life.

St. Francis of Assisi (1181-1226)

Be at peace

Do not look forward to what might happen tomorrow; the same
everlasting Father, who cares for you today, will take care of you
tomorrow and everyday. Either He will shield you from suffering,
or He will give you unfailing strength to bear it. Be at peace then,
and put aside all anxious thoughts and imaginations.

St. Francis de Sales, Bishop of Geneva (1567-1622)

Let the day be one of light

Thou unbegotten God, the Sire,
   And thou, the sole-begotten Son,
Who, with the Spirit's sacred fire,
   Art everlasting, Three in One;
To thee no mortal calls in vain,
   Nor does the lover of the light
Lift up unheard a prayerful strain
Nor blindly seek thy holy height.
Reminded by the rising sun,

To thee our grateful hearts we bring;
With love and praise and orison,
In hymns and songs, we gladly sing.
Lord, let the day be one of light,
Build all our labors unto thee;
Thou, who has brought us out of night,
Keep us in strong sincerity. Amen.

St. Hilary of Poitiers (315-367)

Teach me

Lord Jesus, teach me to be generous; teach me to serve you as you deserve, to give and not to count the cost, to fight and not to heed the wounds, to toil and not to seek for rest, to labour and not to seek reward, except that of knowing that I do your will.

St. Ignatius of Loyola (1491-1556)

Luther's morning prayer

We give thanks to you, heavenly Father, through Jesus Christ your dear Son, that you have protected us through the night from all danger and harm; and we beseech you to preserve and keep us, this day also, from all sin and evil; that in all our thoughts, words and deeds, we may serve and please you. Into your hands we commend our bodies and soul, and all that is ours. Let your holy angel guard us, that the wicked one may have no power over us. Amen.

Martin Luther (1483-1546)

Luther's evening prayer

I thank you, my heavenly Father, through Jesus Christ, your dear Son, that you have graciously kept me this day; and I pray you that you would forgive me all my sins where I have done wrong,

and graciously keep me this night. For into your
hands I commend myself, my body and soul,
and all things. Let your holy angel be with me,
that the wicked one may have no power over me. Amen.

Martin Luther (1483-1546)

The things we pray for

Give us, Lord, a humble, quiet, peaceable, patient, tender and
charitable mind, and in all our thoughts, words and deeds a taste
of the Holy Spirit. Give us, Lord, a lively faith, a firm hope, a
fervent charity, a love of you. Take from us all lukewarmness
in meditation, dullness in prayer. Give us fervor and delight in
thinking of you and your grace, your tender compassion towards
us. The things that we pray for, good Lord, give us grace to labour
for; through Jesus Christ our Lord.

St. Thomas More (1478-1535)

Christ be with me

May the strength of God guide me this day,
and may God's power preserve me.
May the wisdom of God instruct me:
the eye of God watch over me; the ear of God hear me; the word
of God give sweetness to my speech; the hand of God defend me;
and may I follow the way of God.
Christ be with me, Christ before me,
Christ behind me, Christ in me,
Christ beneath me, Christ above me,
Christ on my right, Christ on my left,
Christ where I lie, Christ where I sit, Christ where I arise,
Christ in the heart of everyone who thinks of me,
Christ in the mouth of everyone who speaks to me,
Christ in every eye that sees me,

Christ in every ear that hears me.
  Salvation is of the Lord,
  Salvation is of the Lord,
  Salvation is of the Christ.
May your salvation, O Lord, be ever with us. Amen.
                    attributed to St. Patrick, patron saint of Ireland (389-461)

Day by day

Thanks be to thee, Lord Jesus Christ, for
  all the benefits which thou hast won for us, for
  all the pains and insults which thou hast borne for us.
O most merciful Redeemer, Friend and Brother,
  may we know thee more clearly, love thee more dearly,
  and follow thee more nearly, day by day. Amen.
                              St. Richard of Chichester (1198-1253)

God alone suffices

Let nothing disturb you. Let nothing dismay you.
All things pass. God never changes. Patience
achieves everything. Whoever has God lacks nothing.
God alone suffices. Amen.
                                    St. Teresa of Avila (1515-1582)

I worship you

I worship you, O Christ, and thank you that I have been
  counted worthy to suffer for your name.
Let me grasp the greater crown.
As you showed mercy to Rahab, and received the penitent
  thief, turn not your mercy from me. Amen.
                              St. Theodota of Philippopolis (†c318)

Teach us

Teach us to fix our thoughts on thee, reverently
and with love, so that our prayers are not in vain, but are
acceptable to thee, now and always; through Jesus Christ our
Lord. Amen.

Jane Austen, novelist (1775-1817)

One thing we ask

We must praise your goodness that you have left nothing undone
to draw us to yourself. But one thing we ask of you, our God, not
to cease to work in our improvement. Let us tend towards you, no
matter by what means, and be fruitful in good works, for the sake
of Jesus Christ our Lord. Amen.

Ludwig Van Beethoven, composer (1770-1827)

I cry to you

Oh God, early in the morning I cry to you.
Help me to pray, and to concentrate my thoughts on you:
I cannot do this alone.

In me there is darkness, But with you there is light;
I am lonely, but you do not leave me;
I am feeble in heart, but with you there is help;
I am restless, but with you there is peace.
In me there is bitterness, but with you there is patience;
I do not understand your ways,
but you know the way for me . . .

Restore me to liberty, and enable me so to live now
that I may answer before you and before me,
Lord, whatever this day may bring,
Your name be praised. Amen.

Dietrich Bonhoeffer, theologian (1906-1945)

Slow me down, Lord

Slow me down, Lord.
Ease the pounding of my heart
   by the quieting of my mind.
Steady my hurried pace
   with a vision of the eternal reach of time.
Give me, amidst the confusion of my day,
   the calmness of the everlasting hills.
Break the tension of my nerves and muscles
   with the soothing music of singing streams
   that live in my memories.
Help me to know the magical, restorative power
   of your touch.
Teach me the art of taking minute vacations,
slowing down to look at a flower,
   to chat with a friend,
   to pet a dog.
Remind me each day of the fable of the hare and the tortoise
   so that I may know that the race is not always won
     by the swift.
There is more to life than increasing its speed.
Let me look upward into the branches of the towering oak,
   and know that it grew slowly and well.
Slow me down, Lord.
Inspire me to send my roots deep
   into the soil of life's enduring values.

Richard Cardinal Cushing (1895-1970

In Depression

O God, you care for your creation with great tenderness.
In the midst of the greatest pain, you offer hope.
Give help to me, whose spirit seems to be lost

...nd whose soul is in despair.
...et me feel your pure love.
...et me believe in the miracle of rebirth
...o that I can experience now a small taste of the
...appiness I hope to know in eternity. Amen.

Dimma, an Irish Monk (7th Century)

Open the door of thy church

O Lord God, I have hoped to feel after thee and find thee and
...o know thy mysteries, but I do not understand the church's
...nguage; its customs are strange and always I feel a stranger there.
...Why cannot I find a home in thy church? Search me out where I
...m, O God, and send me brethren in my loneliness. Give to the
...hurch servants who will speak my language and understand me.
Open the door of thy church and help me, O God. Amen.

John W. Doberstein, writer, teacher (1905-1965)

Grant true discernment

Grant, O Lord, to all students, to know what is worth knowing,
...o love what is worth loving, to praise what delights you most,
...o value what is precious in your sight and to reject what is evil
...n your eyes. Grant them true discernment to distinguish between
...ifferent things. Above all, may they search out and do what is
...nost pleasing to you; through Jesus Christ our Lord. Amen.

Thomas à Kempis, monk (1380-1471)

Teach me

Teach me, O God, not to torture myself, not to make a martyr
...ut of myself through stifling reflection, but rather teach me to
...reathe deeply in faith. Amen.

Søren Kierkegaard, philosopher (1813-1855)

Power of endurance

O God, our Heavenly Father,

In these days of emotional tension, when the problems of the world are gigantic in extent and chaotic in detail, give us penetrating vision, broad understanding, power of endurance and abiding faith, and save us from the paralysis of crippling fear. And O God, we ask Thee to help us to work with renewed vigor for a warless world and for a brotherhood that transcends race or color. We ask in the name of him who taught us to pray. Amen
Martin Luther King, Jr., minister, civil rights leader (1929-1968)

Till all my questions cease

O Christ - pour Thy still dews of quietness
Till all my questions cease
Take from my soul the strain and stress
And let my answering life confess
The beauty of Thy peace.
Otto Paul Kretzmann, churchman, writer, educator (1901-1975)

Communion with God

Master, they say that when I seem
    To be in speech with you,
Since you make no replies, it's all a dream
    – One talker aping two.
They are half right, but not as they
    Imagine; rather, I
Seek in myself the things I meant to say,
    And lo! The wells are dry.
Then, seeing me empty, you forsake
    The Listener's role, and through
    My dead lips breathe and into utterance wake

The thoughts I never knew.

And thus you neither need reply
    Nor can; thus, while we seem
Two talking, thou art One forever, and I
    No dreamer, but thy dream.

       C.S. Lewis, Irish author and scholar (1898-1963)

The road ahead

My Lord God,
  I have no idea where I am going.
  I do not see the road ahead of me.
  I cannot know for certain where it will end.
Nor do I really know myself, and the fact
  that I think I am following your will does not mean
  that I am actually doing so.
But I believe that the desire to please you
  does in fact please you.
And I hope I have that desire in all that I am doing.
I hope that I will never do anything
  apart from that desire.
And I know that if I do this you will lead me by the right
  road, though I may know nothing about it.
Therefore, I will trust you always though I may
  seem to be lost in the shadow of death.
I will not fear for you are ever with me
  and you will never leave me to face my perils alone.
       Thomas Merton, Trappist monk and author (1915-1968)

Thank you, Jesus, for bringing me this far

Thank you, Jesus, for bringing me this far.
  In your light, I see the light of my life.
  Your teaching is brief and to the point:

You persuade us to trust in our heavenly Father;
  you command us to love one another.
What is easier than to believe in God?
What is sweeter than to love Him?
Your yoke is pleasant, your burden is light,
  you the only teacher.

You promise everything to those who obey your teaching;
  you ask nothing too hard for a believer,
  nothing a lover can refuse.
Your promises to your disciples are true,
  entirely true, nothing but the truth.
Even more, you promise us yourself,
  the perfection of all that can be made perfect.
Thank you, Jesus, now and always. Amen.

Nicholas of Cusa, Bishop of Brixen (1401-146

Serenity

O God,

You created all things according to your plan.
In this very moment,
I know you guide and govern the world.
Grant me the serenity
  to accept the things I cannot change,
  the courage to change the things I can,
  and the wisdom to know the difference.

Living one day at a time,
  enjoying one moment at a time,
    accepting hardships as a pathway to peace,
  taking as Jesus did,
  this sinful world as it is,
  not as I would have it,
  trusting that you would make all things right

if I surrender to your will,
so that I may be reasonably happy in this life
and supremely happy with you
forever in the next.
I ask this through Christ our Lord. Amen.

Reinhold Niebuhr, theologian (1892-1971)

Help me by my love

Help me, O Lord, to be more loving.

Help me, O Lord, not to be afraid to love the outcast, the leper, the unmarried pregnant woman, the traitor to the State, the man out of prison.

Help me by my love to restore the faith of the disillusioned, the disappointed, the early bereaved.

Help me by my love to be the witness of thy love.
And may I this coming day be able to do some work of peace for Thee. Amen.

Alan Paton, author (1903-1988)

A Christmas wish

Loving Father, help us remember the birth of Jesus, that we may share in the song of the angels, the gladness of the shepherds, and the wisdom of the wise men.

Close the door of hate and open the door of love all over the world. Let kindness come with every gift and good desires with every greeting.

Deliver us from evil by the blessing which Christ brings, and teach us to be merry with clean hearts.

May the Christmas morning make us happy to be thy children, and the Christmas evening bring us to our beds with grateful thoughts, forgiving and forgiven, for Jesus' sake. Amen.

Robert Louis Stevenson, novelist (1850-1894)

Thy people shall be our people

Father, we pray Thee not that Thou shouldest take us out of the world, but we pray Thee to keep us from evil. Give us neither poverty nor riches, feed us with bread convenient for us. And let Thy songs be our delight in the houses of our pilgrimage. God of our Fathers be our God: may their people be our people, their faith our faith. We are strangers on the earth, hide not Thy commandments from us, but may the love of Christ constrain us. Entreat us not to leave Thee or refrain from following Thee. Thy people shall be our people; Thou shalt be our God. Amen.

Vincent Van Gogh, artist (1853-1890

Deliver me, I pray

O God, who has called me to place such complete trust in you that nothing can tyrannize my life,
deliver me, I pray…

   from becoming a slave to my books
   from daydreaming away my time
   from an overconcern about sex
   from an overanxiety about my future
   from an uncritical view of myself
   from an overcritical view of myself

and from all the half-known deities which try to dictate what I shall be. Save me, that I may be free to make responsible decisions and serve you with wholeness. Amen.

John W. Vannorsdall, author (b.1924

Renewing the face of the world

O God, Creator of all things, you are perpetually renewing the face of the world and have created us new in Jesus Christ; grant that in our worship of you and in communion with you, your

created energy may more and more flood
our lives, so that we may play our part in the
fulfillment of your purpose, which transcends
all that we can think or understand. Amen.

Willem Adolf Visser 't Hooft, theologian (1900-1985)

Holy Scriptures

Blessed Lord, who has caused all Holy Scriptures to be written
for our learning, grant that we may in such wise hear them, read,
mark, and learn, and inwardly digest them, that by patience and
comfort of the Holy Word, we may embrace and ever hold fast the
blessed hope of everlasting life, which thou hast given us in our
Saviour Jesus Christ. Amen.

Book of Common Prayer

Good Lord, deliver us

From the cowardice that dare not face new truth,
from the laziness that is contented with half truth,
from the arrogance that thinks it knows all truth,
good Lord, deliver me. Amen.

Kenyan prayer

Give us faith

Lord God, you have called your servants to ventures of which
we cannot see the ending, by paths as yet untrodden, through
perils unknown. Give us faith to go out with good courage, not
knowing where we go, but only that your hand is leading us and
your love supporting us; through Jesus Christ our Lord. Amen.

Lutheran Book of Worship, Evening Prayer: Vespers

Give me someone

Lord Jesus,

When I am famished, give me someone who needs food.
When I am thirsty, send me someone who needs water.
When I am cold, send me someone to warm.
When I am hurting, send me someone to console.
When my cross becomes heavy, give me another's cross to share.
When I am poor, lead someone needy to me.
When I have no time, give me someone to help for a moment.
When I am humiliated, give me someone to praise.
When I am discouraged, send me someone to encourage.
When I need another's understanding, give me someone
   who needs mine.
When I need somebody to take care of me, send me someone
   to care for.
When I think of myself, turn my thoughts toward another.
And when I think I can make no difference in the lives of others,
   show me the limitless possibility of Christ's compassionate
   journey within me.

Author unknown

> ❝ I don't know what your destiny will be,
> but one thing I know: the only ones among you
> who will be really happy are those who have
> sought and found how to serve.
>
> – *Albert Schweitzer, humanitarian,*
> *theolgian, doctor (1875-1965)* ❞

May your bounty teach me

Lord,

Isn't your creation wasteful? Fruits never equal the seedings' abundance.

Springs scatter water. The sun gives out enormous light.

May your bounty teach me greatness of heart.

May your magnificence stop me being mean.

Seeing you a prodigal and open-handed giver
let me give unstintingly
like a king's son

Like God's own. Amen.

> Helder Pessoa Camara, archbishop, theologian (1909-1999)

Creator, create anew love within me

When I sit in the darkness of meditation,
even the darkness and coldness of prison,
quietly…
my life communicates with God.

He whispers within when other forms
of communication are lost.

I see him within
when outerness is darkness.

Creator, create anew love within me,
broken am I; begin thy repairing.

The triumph is this:
God, through my consciousness,
begins a new world-reformation. Amen.

> Toyohiko Kagawa, Japanese social reformer (1888-1960)

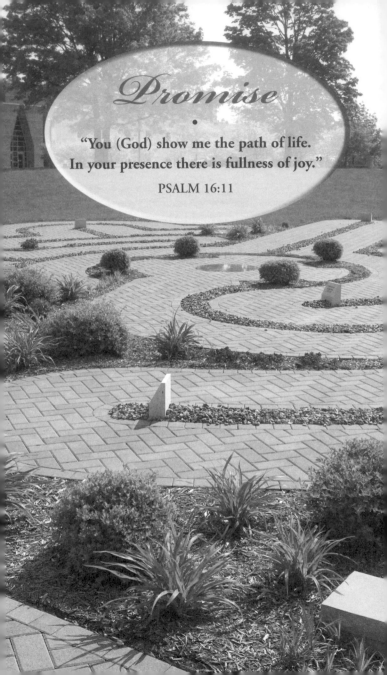

Promise

·

"You (God) show me the path of life.
In your presence there is fullness of joy."

PSALM 16:11

Purpose – Life is a spiritual journey. Faith and worship grow out of the story of God and God's people moving through time. Walking a path, whether a forest trail, a bike path, a labyrinth or the way you usually go home, can offer a refreshing means to talk with God in prayer.

Practice – Since the disciples' encounter with the resurrected Jesus on their way to Emmaus, meaning is given to prayerful walks. For example, the labyrinth represents a journey to our own center and back again into the world. Labyrinths have long been used as meditation and prayer tools through the ages.

Process

1. **Focus:** Become quiet and think of God. Give a bow, nod, or other gesture and begin your walk or enter the labyrinth.

2. **Experience:** Walk purposefully. Listen to God. When you reach the center or destination, stay there and focus several moments. Leave and return when it seems appropriate.

3. **Exit:** When your walk ends. Give an acknowledgement of ending, such as "Amen."

4. **Reflect:** After walking the path, reflect back on your experience.

5. **Walk often.**

Prayer – Give thanks to Jesus who walks with you, thanking him for his continued presence and companionship.

Consideration prayer

Lord,
help me to consider
that everyone has the right:
    to be considered,
    to be consulted,
    to be listened to,
    to be appreciated,
    to be noticed,
    to make mistakes,
    to be forgiven,
    to be allowed
    to start once again!

Lord,
help me to realize
that everyone has the right:
    not to be ignored,
    not to be insulted,
    not to shut up,
    not to be shut out,
    not to be neglected,
    not to be rejected,
    not to be abused,
    not to be refused
    a second chance!

Holy Family College. *Holy Family College Prayerbook*, 1994

Student government prayer

Keep us, O Lord, from pettiness. Let us be large in thought, in word, in deed. Let us be done with fault-finding and leave off with self-seeking. May we put away all pretense and meet each other face-to-face without pity and without prejudice.

May we never be hasty in judgment, and always generous. Teach us to put into action our better impulses, straightforward and unafraid.

Let us take time for all things. May we grow calm, serene, and gentle. Grant that we may realize that it is the little things that create difference; that in the big things of life we are as one. And may we strive to touch and know the great common heart of us all.

And oh, Lord, let us not forget to be kind.

Mary, Queen of Scots (1542-1587)
Holy Family College. *Holy Family College Prayerbook*, 1994.

Runner's prayer

Run by my side—live in my heartbeat;
  give strength to my steps.
As the cold confronts me,
  as the wind pushes me,
    I know you surround me.
As the sun warms me,
  as the rain cleanses me,
    I know you are touching me,
    challenging me,
    loving me.
And so I give you this run;
thank you for matching my stride. Amen.

University of Notre Dame. *The Day Awaits*, 1997.

Sending blessing for student service volunteers

Lord,
We ask you to bless and keep these people safe
  as they travel across our country
    to other lands.

Keep them safe from harm.

Let their days be filled
      with the joy of compassion,
   their communities mindful of your call,
   their minds focused on the gifts they have and are,
   and their hearts aware of your workings
      through their actions.

We ask you to bless those whom they will serve,
      those closest to you,
   the children, the poor, the sick, the homeless,
      and all who call witness to Christ's presence
            here on earth.

Bless their nights
      with the anticipation of the morning,
   and the glory of your resurrection.

We ask this through Christ's name. Amen.

University of Notre Dame. *The Day Awaits*, 1997.

Before a performance

Dear Lord,

I am here by your grace.
My talents grow from what you have given me.
Thank you for those gifts.
I have worked hard to prepare for this moment.
Thank you for the energy and time to do that.
You will help me through any challenge.
Thank you for your loving support.
I surrender to your care.
Thank you.
I'll do my best.

Sacred Heart University. *Prayers from the Heart,* 2002

When I cannot pray

When I cannot pray, let me be silent.
If I cannot be silent, let me ask "Lord, where are you when
I need you?"
When no answer comes to satisfy my weary heart, let me have the
courage to be like Job, to raise my hands towards the heavens and
scream, "What gives?"
If I do not hear your voice, let me hope.
If hope is more than I can manage,
then let me be silent.
When I can no longer be silent,
Lord, help me to pray. Amen.

Sacred Heart University. *Prayers from the Heart*, 2002.

An administrator's prayer

When I have too much to do,
help me to turn to you, my God.
Give me insight into what is important at this moment —
grant me courage to face challenges . . .
compassion as I listen to others . . .
perseverance to tackle difficult tasks . . .
peace in all things. Above all, help me, my God, to remember that
it is your work that I am about – not mine. Amen.

Sacred Heart University. *Prayers from the Heart*, 2002.

A prayer of surrender

My dear and glorious God,

I must confess that for some time I have tried to do things
my own way.
I have fought against You, and what You try to have me
do for You.
But in doing this I have grown tired, cold, and jaded.

203

All I can do now is just surrender.
You have destroyed the walls to my heart, and I cannot
    stop You from invading my soul.
May your light shine through me, your tenderness fill me,
your empathy wash over me, and your love strengthen me
as I start down the quest you send me on.
Please always be at my side, and allow me
to follow You to my true home with You.

St. Norbert College. *One Mind, One Heart in God*, 2003.

Prayer for the oppressed

O God,

I pray for oppressed people everywhere.
The injustices I see among the people
of the world toward one another, and at times,
find even in myself, rise from our failure
to appreciate and recognize our fellowship.
Grant peace and security
to those who are poor, aged, sick, or disabled,
and those who suffer from the ravages of war
and the natural disasters of the earth.
Grant us the wisdom to deal honestly
and uprightly with people
of all races and cultures.
Help us to overcome the prejudices
we harbor within ourselves.
Help me to realize the equality of all people
in their rights to life, freedom, and happiness
in this world and in the next.
May I do my part to recognize and serve you in
my brothers and sisters. Amen.

St. Francis Xavier University. *Prayers for the Xaverian Family*, 2003

Prayer in time of conflict

Gentle me, Holy One,
into an unclenched moment, a deep breath,
a letting go of heavy experiences,
of shriveling anxieties, of dead certainties, that,
softened by the silence,
surrounded by the light,
and open to the mystery,
I may be found by wholeness, upheld by the
unfathomable, entranced by the simple,
and filled with the joy that is You. Amen.

St. Francis Xavier University. *Prayers for the Xaverian Family*, 2003.

For a light in the darkness

Father, grant that I may be
a bearer of Christ Jesus, your son.
Allow me to warm the often cold, impersonal
scene of modern life with your burning love.
Strengthen me, by your Holy Spirit
to carry out my mission of changing the world
or some definite part of it, for the better.
Despite my lamentable failures, bring home to me
that my advantages are your blessings
to be shared with others.
Make me more energetic in setting to rights
what I find wrong with the world
instead of complaining about it or myself.
Nourish in me a practical desire
to build up rather than tear down
to reconcile more than polarize
to go out on a limb rather than crave security.
Never let me forget that it is far better
to light one candle than to curse the darkness.
And to join my light, one day, with yours. Amen.

University of Notre Dame. *Day by Day*, 2004.

For good attitudes toward sex

Sometimes I feel like I am going crazy.
I've got all this sex-drive going in me,
pounding in me, burning in me, tantalizing me.
It delights and yet disturbs me;
it confuses and bewilders me.
What I do about it often bothers me
and makes me feel rotten about myself.

How should I think about sex, Lord?
How should I express my growing sexuality?
What is the real truth about sex and sexual love?
In the Creed we say you are the creator of heaven and earth
and that your son actually took flesh for our sake;
you must know more about sex than we do!
Sex must be a part of your lovely plan for us,
and since your son became a sexual being like us
the truth about sex must come from
a deeper, fuller understanding of the Word-made-flesh
who came and dwelt among us.

In my confusion make me realize, first of all,
that sex is one of your finest gifts.
Being afraid of it or being ashamed of it
is no way to thank you for it!
Because my sexuality is your personal gift to me,
help me to accept it graciously and to use it thankfully,
with full human responsibility. And that is asking a lot!

University of Notre Dame. *Day by Day*, 2004

A prayer for college students

God has created me to do some definite service;
God has committed some work to me
    which has not been committed to another.
I have my mission—I may never know it in this life,
    but I shall be told it in the next.

I am a link in the chain,
   a bond of connection between persons.
God has not created me for naught.
I shall do good.
I shall do God's work.
I shall be an angel of peace,
   a preacher of truth in my own place.
Whatever, wherever I am,
   I can never be thrown away.
If I am in sickness, my sickness may serve the Lord;
   in perplexity, my perplexity may serve the Lord;
      if I am in sorrow, my sorrow may serve the Lord.
God does nothing in vain.
Therefore I will trust in the Lord. Amen.
      University of Notre Dame. *Lead, Kindly Light*, 2005.

Lead, kindly Light

Lead kindly Light, amid the encircling gloom,
   Lead Thou me on!

The night is dark, and I am far from home –
   Lead Thou me on!

Keep Thou my feet; I do not ask to see
The distant scene—one step enough for me.

I was not ever thus, nor prayed that Thou
   Shouldst lead me on.
I loved to choose and see my path; but now,
   Lead Thou me on!
I loved the garish day, and, spite of fears,
Pride ruled my will: remember not past year.

So long Thy power hath blessed me,
sure it still will lead me on,
O'er moor and fen, o'er crag and torrent, till
   The night is gone;
And with the morn those angel faces smile
Which I have loved long since, and lost awhile.
            John Henry Cardinal Newman (1801-1890)
         University of Notre Dame. *Lead, Kindly Light*, 2005.

On-campus Prayer Partners

Chapel of the Resurrection:
http://www.valpo.edu/chapel/worship.php

Fellowship of Christian Athletes:
http://www.valpo.edu/student/fca/

InterVarsity for Christian Fellowship:
http://www.valpo.edu/organization/ivcf/

Lutheran Deaconess Association:
http://www.valpo.edu/lda/

St. Teresa of Avila Catholic Student Center:
http://www.valpo.edu/student/stt/

University Prayer Books

The Day Awaits. Ed. John and Sylvia Dillon. Indiana: University of Notre Dame Campus Ministry, 1997.

Day by Day. Ed. Thomas McNally and William Storey. Notre Dame, Indiana: Ave Maria Press, 2004.

Holy Family College Prayer Book. Ed. Moya R. Kaporch. Philadelphia, PA, 1994.

Little Red Book. Center for Ignatian Spirituality. Newton, Massachusetts: Boston College, 2002.

Lead, Kindly Light. Ed. John and Sylvia Dillon. Indiana: University of Notre Dame Campus Ministry, 2005.

One Mind, One Heart in God. St. Norbert College Mission & Heritage Office. Wisconsin: Independent, Inc., 2003.

Our Hope for Years to Come: Valparaiso University Prayer Book. Ed. Gail McGrew Eifrig and Frederick Niedner. Indiana: Valparaiso University Press, 2001.

University Prayer Books (con't)

Prayers for the Xaverian Family. The Chaplaincy
Office of St. Francis Xavier University. Nova Scotia, Canada:
The Casket Printing and Publishing Company, Ltd., 2003.

Prayers from the Heart. Ed. Patricia Leonard Pasley. Fairfield,
Connecticut: Sacred Heart University Press, 2002.

Prayer Books for Devotional Use

*Celtic Daily Prayers: Prayers and Readings From the Northumbria
Community.* New York: HarperCollins Publishers, Inc., 2002.

For All The Saints, Volumes I-IV. Ed. Frederick J. Schumacher.
New York: American Lutheran Publicity Bureau, 2005.

Collins, Owen. *2,000 Years of Classic Christian Prayers.* Maryknoll,
NY: Orbis Books, 1999.

Doberstein, John. *A Lutheran Prayer Book.* Philadelphia:
Muhlenberg Press, 1960.

Episcopal Church, The. *The Book of Common Prayer.*

Philip Pfatteicher. *The Daily Prayer of the Church.* Minneapolis,
Minnesota: Lutheran University Press, 2005.

Shawchuck, Norman and Job, Rueben. *A Guide to Prayer for All
Who Seek God.* Nashville, TN: Upper Room Publishing, 2006.

Books about Prayer

Augustine of Hippo, St. *The Confessions of St. Augustine.* Ada, MI:
Baker Publishing Group, 2007.

Bonhoeffer, Dietrich. *The Cost of Discipleship.* New York: Simon
& Schuster, 1995.

Brueggemann, Walter. *Awed to Heaven, Rooted in Earth.*
Minneapolis, MN: Fortress Press, 2003.

Books about Prayer (con't)

Card, Michael. *A Sacred Sorrow: Reaching Out to God in the Lost Language of Lament.* Colorado Springs, CO: NavPress Publishing Group, 2005.

Foster, Richard. *Prayer.* San Francisco, CA: HarperSanFrancisco, 2007.

Harper, Steve. *Talking in the Dark.* Nashville, TN: The Upper Room, 2006.

Hauerwas, Stanley. *Prayers Plainly Spoken.* Eugene, OR: Wipf & Stock Publishers, 2003.

Indermark, John. *Traveling the Prayer Paths of Jesus.* Nashville, TN: Upper Room Publishing, 2003.

Jones, Tony. *Pray.* Colorado Springs, CO: NavPress, 2003.

Lockyer, Herbert. *All the Prayers of the Bible.* Grand Rapids, MI: Zondervan, 1990.

Nesser, Joann. *Contemplative Prayer, Praying When the Well Runs Dry.* Minneapolis, MN: Augsburg Books, 2007.

Nouwen, Henri J. M. *The Only Necessary Thing, Living a Prayerful Life.* New York: Crossroad Publishing, 1999.

Wangerin Jr., Walter. *Whole Prayer: Speaking & Listening to God.* Grand Rapids, MI: Zondervan, 1998.

Westphal, Merold. *Not About Me: Prayer is the Work of a Lifetime*, pp. 20-25. Nashville, TN: Upper Room Publishing, 2005.

Wolpert, Daniel. *Creating a Life with God: The Call of Ancient Prayer Practices.* Nashville, TN: Upper Room Publishing,2003.

Yancey, Philip. *Prayer: Does It Make Any Difference?* Grand Rapids, MI: Zondervan, 2006.

—. *Prayer.* Grand Rapids, MI: Zondervan, 2007.

Online resources

www.breathfreshair.org

www.boiler-rooms.com

www.cph.org

www.cptryon.org/prayer/index.html

www.elca.org/prayer

www.faithandworship.com/prayers.htm

www.faithwriters.com/article.php

www.houseofprayer.org.au

www.iona.org.uk/

www.invitationtoprayer.org/index.html

www.lcms.org

www.ocf.org/OrthodoxPage/prayers/index.html

www.oremus.org

www.religion-online.org/

www.sacredspace.ie/

www.staygreat.com/

www.taize.fr

www.universalis.com

www.upperroom.org/methodx/thelife/prayermethods/

www.ycvf.org/oremus

www.yenra.net/catholic/prayers/

SPECIAL ACKNOWLEDGEMENTS

We are grateful to the authors and publishers who have given permission to include material copyrighted or controlled by them.

Names of prayer titles for this collection refer to titles used by the editor. This section constitutes a continuation of the copyright page.

Chapter I

Permission to use these morning and evening prayers was given by Dr. Frederick Niedner, professor of theology, Valparaiso University.

Chapter II

From *A Prayerbook for Husbands and Wives* by Ruthanne and Walther Wangerin, Jr. copyright © 2000 Ruthanne and Walter Wangerin, Jr., admin Augsburg Fortress Press. Used by permission. p. 62.

Prayers from *Evangelical Lutheran Worship*. Copyright © 2006, by permission of Augsburg Fortress. p. 105.

Prayers from *Lutheran Book of Worship*. Copyright © 1978, by permission of Augsburg Fortress. p. 106, 110, 111.

Chapter III: Taking our cares to the Light

The 17 devotionals focused on student issues are used with permission of Rev. James Wetzstein, associate university pastor and associate dean of the Chapel of the Resurrection of Valparaiso University.

Chapter IV: Following the Light...seasons of the church year

The 24 devotionals reflecting the various seasons of the church year are used with permission of Dr. George C. Heider, associate professor of theology, Valparaiso University.

Prayers from *Lutheran Book of Worship*. Copyright © 1978, by permission of Augsburg Fortress. p. 153.

Chapter V: Much-loved expressions of the Light

15 lines from 'Proslogion' (p. 243) taken from THE PRAYERS AND MEDITATIONS OF SAINT ANSELM WITH THE PROSLOGION translated with an introduction by Sister Benedicta Ward, with a forward by R. W. Southern (Penguin Classics, 1973). Copyright © Benedicta Ward, 1973. Foreword copyright © R. W. Southern, 1973. Reproduced by permission of Penguin Books Ltd. p. 181.

From *The Prayers of Catherine of Siena*. 2nd edition, trans., ed. Susanne Noffke, O.P. San Jose: Authors Choice Press, 2001. Used with permission. p. 182.

Excerpt from "Teach me" from *The Prayers of Kierkegaard*. Ed. Perry La Ferve 1978 University of Chicago Press. Used with permission. p. 189.

Prayer taken from *Campus Prayers for the '70s* by John W. Vannorsdall, copyright © 1970 Fortress Press. Used by permission of Augsburg Fortress. p. 194

SPECIAL ACKNOWLEDGEMENTS

Prayers from *Lutheran Book of Worship*. Copyright © 1978, by permission of Augsburg Fortress. p. 195.

Chapter VI: Light from other universities

Excerpts from *Holy Family College Prayerbook*, 1994. Used with permission. p. 200, 201.

Selections are reprinted from *Prayers from the Heart: The Sacred Heart University Prayerbook* © 2002 by Sacred Heart University, Fairfield, Connecticut. Used with permission. All rights reserved. p. 202, 203

Prayer from *One Mind, One Heart in God*, 2003. Used by permission from St. Norbert College. p. 203.

Prayers used by permission from Campus Ministry, University of Notre Dame, Student Book of Prayer © 1997, 2005. p. 201, 206, 207.

Prayers excerpted from *Day by Day* edited by William G. Storey, D.M.S. and Thomas McNally, C.S.C. Copyright © 1975 by Ave Maria Press, P.O. Box 428 Notre Dame, IN 46556, www.avemariapress.com. Used with permission of the publisher. p. 205, 206.

Permission to use the six "ways to pray," noted under **Seeking the Light in Prayer,** and appearing at the front of each chapter, was granted by Rev. Joseph Cunningham, dean of the Chapel of the Resurrection and university pastor of Valparaiso University.

The fine photographic work of Kara Felde Koschmann and Jon L. Hendricks is evident in the full-page and corner photos of this prayer book.

> **" Prayer does not blind us to the world, but it transforms our vision of the world and makes us see it, all people and all the history of humanity in the light of God.**
>
> *Thomas Merton, Trappist monk and author (1915-1968)*

God created us in his image, and we decided to return the favor.

George Bernard Shaw, Irish playwright (1856-1950)

A dehumanized Jesus is a dehumanized God-with-us that gives us license to customize a life of love entirely to our own convenience, without involving us in sacrifice or patience.

Eugene Peterson, pastor, author (1932-   ) **"**

Those people
for whom I wish to pray...

_____

_____

_____

_____

_____

_____

_____

_____

_____

_____

_____

_____

_____

_____

_____

Those people
for whom I wish to pray...

_____

_____

_____

_____

_____

_____

_____

_____

_____

_____

_____

_____

_____

_____

KEY TO PHOTOS BY TITLE, LOCATION, AND PAGE

KEY TO PHOTOS BY TITLE, LOCATION, AND PAGE

INDEX OF PRAYERS BY TITLE, AUTHOR, AND PAGE

All prayers not ascribed to a person in this index, or in the book, were written by the editor.

INDEX OF PRAYERS BY TITLE, AUTHOR, AND PAGE

Hear God's blessing in the Light

May the God of steadfastness and encouragement grant you to live in harmony with one another, in accordance with Christ Jesus, so that together you may with one voice glorify the God and Father of our Lord Jesus Christ.

(Romans 15:5-6)

Now may our Lord Jesus Christ himself and God our Father, who loved us and through grace gave us eternal comfort and good hope, comfort your hearts and strengthen them in every good work and word.

(2 Thessalonians 2:16-17)

And the peace of God, which surpasses all understanding, will guard your hearts and your minds in Christ Jesus.

(Philippians 4:7)

The grace of the Lord Jesus Christ, the love of God, and the communion of the Holy Spirit be with all of you.

(2 Corinthians 13:13)

APPRECIATIONS AND THANKS

For two years a very remarkable and dedicated group of students advised the editor on a host of prayer book issues. Among their number: Renee Brozo, Kevin Clemens, Erin Dalpini, Marcus Lohrmann, Steve Miller, James Nagel, Beth Niggemyer, Leah Parker, Jamie Petitto, Andrew Stoebig, and Emily Weller. Their contributions have been substantial and stellar. May they be edified by the fruits of their labor.

Special thanks to Kara Felde Koschmann ('07) and Mark Koschmann ('07), co-conveners of the advisory team, whose perspective and leadership greatly enriched the book you hold in your hand.

Appreciations are also in order to:

- Elly (Schroeder) Boerke ('05) and Daniella Trombatore ('05) who implemented the first prayer book survey.

- James Old, who provided the student advisory team with readable survey results on two occasions.

- Karl Aho ('07), who identified other university prayer books as well as an array of other prayer resources.

- The host of faculty and staff who took time on a Sunday afternoon to talk with the advisory team about prayer in their lives.

- Those 145 faculty, staff, students, and alumni who willingly submitted original prayers or who shared their perspectives on "Prayer is…".

- Pastors Joseph Cunningham, George C. Heider, Fred Niedner, and James Wetzstein, who each crafted a section of this prayer book.

- Kathy Wehling, Jon L. Hendricks ('01), Becca Spivak Hendricks, Gail Kemper, Fred Niedner, Joseph Cunningham, and Joanne Albers, whose refinement efforts helped bring the book to publication.

- Susan Collins, whose keen eye and gracious spirit assisted the editor in refining numerous drafts of the Prayer Book.

- Michele Karpenko ('67) for her clear, candid, and careful counsel during the final stages of editing this book.

- The Valparaiso University Guild and its director, Julie Thomas ('95), for their gracious financial support and inspiring mission.

Amen

amen

All shall be Amen and Alleluia.
We shall rest and we shall see.
We shall see and we shall know.
We shall know and we shall love.
We shall love and we shall praise.
Behold our end which is no end. Amen.

St. Augustine (354-430)